Sought Through
Prayer and Meditation

Sought Through
Prayer and Meditation

Wisdom from the Sunday 11th Step Meetings
at the Wolfe Street Center in Little Rock

Geno W.
with William G. Borchert

Hazelden
Publishing

Hazelden Publishing
Center City, Minnesota 55012
hazelden.org/bookstore

Library of Congress Cataloging-in-Publication Data

W., Geno.
Sought through prayer and meditation : wisdom from the Sunday
11th step meetings at the Wolfe Street Center in Little Rock /
Geno W. with William G. Borchert.
        p. cm.
Includes bibliographical references (p.   ).
ISBN 978-1-59285-658-9 (softcover)
1. Twelve step programs—Religious aspects—Meditations.
I. Borchert, William G. II. Title.
BL624.5.W214 2008
204'.42—dc22
                                                2008035009

Editor's note
The names, details, and circumstances may have been changed
to protect the privacy of those mentioned in this publication.
Alcoholics Anonymous, AA, and the Big Book are registered
trademarks of Alcoholics Anonymous World Services, Inc.

22   8

Cover design by David Swanson
Interior design and typesetting by David Swanson

Contents

Testimonials

I first met Geno W. in Little Rock through my friend and partner in recovery, Joe McQuany. I do not believe that the Wolfe Street Foundation would have become what it is, nor could it have helped the number of people that it has, without Geno's support and guidance. I thank God for Geno and the others at Wolfe Street over the years who have given so freely of their time and expertise and made the wisdom captured in this book possible.

—Charlie P.

I knew Geno well for a number of years before his passing. He visited me in Los Angeles on occasion, and I saw him in Little Rock. I was surprised, however, when he asked me to be his sponsor. I felt mixed emotions about this. I was honored that he had chosen me, but realized I had lost a friend, since my role would have to be a bit different. It turned out that we had a successful experience nevertheless, and his passing left a hole in my heart.

—Clancy I.

Through much prayer, study, and meditation, Geno shared his insights and wisdom with all those at the Hour of Power meeting at the Wolfe Street Center in Little Rock. He also loved to come to Rose City for our Big Book Study, and we would share our thoughts, experiences, programs, beliefs, and spiritual insights with one another. Geno had a thirst for God consciousness and lived his beliefs. As a member of Al-Anon, I was blessed to call him friend, and I miss him.

—Mary Pearl

Geno was unique—a kind of cross between Goldfinger and Father Christmas. He made me do all the stuff that I needed but didn't want to do—just the right guy for me at the right time. I will always be grateful to him.

—Phillip M.

Geno believed that secrets killed us. That's why when he was first diagnosed with cancer, he told all his friends that he was scared. He told us God was with him. He told us he would keep doing what he knew worked. He then told the entire Hour of Power gathering. He talked of it often while he could still lead a meeting. Once he said: "When I was diagnosed with cancer, I thought, well, that's okay. God will use me to show others how to get through something like this with dignity. I won't be afraid. I won't be sniffly. I won't be sorry for myself and I won't slip into despair." As a member of Al-Anon, he taught me so much about how to live and how to die with grace and dignity.

—Cindy H.

The feeling of community that Geno fostered supported a sense of welcome, comfort, encouragement, and nonjudgmental consolation that became a source of strength for all in good times and in bad. Through his patient encouragement I gradually developed a voice to express aspects of my journey in recovery, particularly as it related to prayer and meditation. I became very close to Geno and, in a relationship that continued until his death, was privileged to share a great many special times with him and learn much through the Hour of Power meetings.

—Jim W.

The Sunday morning Hour of Power was my favorite group. It always gave me inspiration to keep on trudging. Geno would bring all his experience into the meeting and use his experience to help people in ways to which an eighth-grade-educated person or a scholar could relate. He told me early on that I should pray on my knees even if I didn't want to because on my knees I wouldn't be giving God any orders.

—Michael S.

I had moved to another town in Mississippi, and one night while at work a loud knock came on the office door. I had been feeling alone and isolated for several weeks. I answered the door and there was Geno W. He said no one had heard from me in Little Rock for several months. He said he was passing through town on business and decided to look me up because he had been praying for me and was concerned. We spent most of the night talking about God, and we never lost touch again. None of my drinking buddies had ever shown that kind of concern about me. He appeared in my life when I needed someone, and I believe God sent him.

—J. G. R.

Geno W. has had a dynamic impact on my life, as God used him to help me recover from this disease. I first met him at the Hour of Power meeting in January of 1984. We met downstairs at Wolfe Street and cooked breakfast before the meeting, as we do today upstairs.

After several unsuccessful attempts at recovery over the next few years, I was being taken drunk to a meeting on Thursday, March 31, 1988, and was asked to run into the YMCA to pick someone up and ran into Geno. I asked him to be my sponsor, and the next twelve years, until his death, he and I enjoyed a relationship few people encounter. He was hard on me in the beginning and required me to do a lot of things he knew I didn't want to do. It was by following his suggestions in spite of me that I realized I can get and stay sober. My sobriety date is April 1, 1988. Although he sponsored a lot of people, he always made time for me and was always there when I needed him most. He had a way of hitting you with what he called "a two-by-four of truth" to get me to see past the "my case is different" and other lies our disease will try to get us to believe. He continually reminded me to live in the moment and that our disease works by having us "think the lie, believe the lie, and when we take the ultimate act of rebellion, [letting the lie] kill us when we try and live the lie."

Geno started having me chair the Hour of Power meeting over the years and, through his "spies at the meeting," would tell me when I did a good job and would tell me to keep up my spiritual connection. In fact, for every New Year's resolution, he would tell me to list at the top "a burning desire to improve my conscious contact with God." I had no idea at the time he was setting me up to carry on the tradition of chairing the meeting after his death. He knew it would be difficult for one person to be there every Sunday, so it was divided up weekly, with one person chairing the first Sunday of the month, another chairing the second Sunday of the month (which I chair), and so on. This tradition of chairing the Hour of Power meeting continues on to this day.

It is by trying to give back what has been so freely given to me that I realize how much Geno has positively influenced my recovery and my life. His unselfishness and desire to help others recover motivate me to emulate him and carry the message to others. He will always be remembered, and I am grateful I had a chance to thank him and tell him I loved him right before he died.

—Bob O.

Introduction

In our daily practice of prayer and meditation, how often have we been moved by a particular thought or postulate, something that touched us deeply? In that special moment, our soul was swayed, our spiritual aura and insight uplifted, only to have that marvelous experience drift from our consciousness a short time later and be gone completely before day's end.

Perhaps if that same thought or concept were there in our next day's meditation and the day after that, we would more likely be able to savor its insight in even greater depth. This could then provide the opportunity for such an experience to become a true wellspring for our spiritual condition, a sturdy linchpin in our recovery from alcoholism.

This special book, based on the chronicles from the Hour of Power Eleventh Step meditation meetings originated and conducted by Geno W., cofounder of the well-known Wolfe Street Center in Little Rock, Arkansas, is designed to provide just such an opportunity. It offers spiritual thoughts and postulates that can be meditated on for an entire week, thus giving the reader the occasion to probe deeply into the awesome power of the Eleventh Step of Alcoholics Anonymous and other Twelve Step programs.

It is, in a sense, patterned after the Twelve Step program of Alcoholics Anonymous itself, in which constant repetition of its concepts and principles builds a strong foundation for sobriety. So too can the thoughtful repetition of specific spiritual concepts reinforce that foundation and enable one to build a strong spiritual life based on a "conscious contact with God as we understood Him"—the only certain solution to the disease of alcoholism.

The purpose of this book, then, is to enhance our practice of the Eleventh Step in our daily prayers and meditation. If we are vigilant in that pursuit, the program of AA promises we will soon see a glimpse of that ultimate reality, which is the kingdom of God.

Wolfe Street and the Hour of Power

Each year, more than a hundred thousand men and women cross the threshold of the Wolfe Street Center in Little Rock, Arkansas, hoping to find some semblance of peace and serenity in their troubled worlds. They have this hope of a daily reprieve thanks to three recovered alcoholics who dedicated much of their lives to helping others.

It was in the fall of 1982 when Geno W., Joe McQuanny, and Bert Jones, three local businessmen who have since passed on, saw the need for a place that could provide frequent support meetings for those seeking recovery from alcoholism through the program of Alcoholics Anonymous. They found a former nurses' residence at 1210 Wolfe Street and, with the assistance of volunteers, turned the two-story building into a comfortable facility where today AA groups hold more than forty meetings each week and where a variety of special activities and special events support and celebrate recovery.

As the Center grew as a focal point of sobriety, its founders and new board of directors created an outreach program to carry the message of recovery from addiction into jails and prisons, courts and corporations, and other community organizations eager to learn more about combating this growing problem.

Today, the Wolfe Street Center actively implements Twelve Step programs designed to educate and help all those seeking recovery from addiction, including families whose problems relate to alcoholism.

Convinced that the real answer lies in focusing on the spiritual solution fostered by the founders of Alcoholics Anonymous, in 1983 Geno W. proposed the institution of a special meeting at the Center specifically for that purpose—to help himself and others find greater spiritual awareness and growth through meditating on AA's Eleventh Step: "Sought through prayer and meditation to improve our conscious contact with God *as we understood Him,* praying only for knowledge of His will for us and the power to carry that out."

That meeting, which he called "The Hour of Power," is still held every Sunday morning at the Center from 10:00 to 11:00 a.m. It's one of the largest meetings of its kind in Little Rock and very much a major commitment for all the groups that meet at the Wolfe Street Center.

Many of those who were close to Geno W. personally recall with great warmth and appreciation his unstinting preparations for each Eleventh Step gathering. He would rise between 3:00 and 4:00 in the morning—the time he often described as "those hours of desperation" for most drunks, when God has a chance of touching their hearts—and start making notes for that morning's meditation meeting.

His topics usually centered on ways of establishing and improving "our conscious contact with God" and on how pain can open the door, how humility can create the pathway, how prayer can light the way, and how true faith can establish a strong personal relationship with our Higher Power. It was the accumulation of these notes chronicled on yellow pads that provide the basis and direction for this book.

After finishing his notations, Geno would arrive at the Center around six to team up with his breakfast crew. While he never said so himself, once again those who knew him said his cooking and serving breakfast to all those who came for the Hour of Power meeting gave him the humility he needed to share his most intimate spiritual thoughts and lead others toward a greater dedication to, and practice of, the Eleventh Step.

It is the hope of all those at the Wolfe Street Center that you, the reader, gain as much insight from Geno W.'s meditation topics and concepts as they continue to gain from each and every Hour of Power meeting.

Mission Statement of the Wolfe Street Foundation

The mission of the Wolfe Street Foundation, Inc., is to provide facilities for support groups faithful to the original Twelve Steps of Alcoholics Anonymous and to develop and implement programs aimed toward education and prevention for those persons interested in recovery from addictions and for their families as they relate to alcoholism.

The Wolfe Street Center is owned and operated by the Wolfe Street Foundation, Inc. The Foundation is a nonprofit, tax-exempt charitable corporation governed by a twelve- to twenty-four-member board, which is not associated with Alcoholics Anonymous or any branch organizations in any form.

Beginning the Journey

The very first word in the Eleventh Step of the program of Alcoholics Anonymous suggests that I be a seeker, a seeker on a journey to discover the awesome power of God that can reconstruct my life. I am urged to begin my journey by asking him to direct my thinking, so that it be free from self-pity and from dishonest and self-seeking motives. I am to ask not only for the strength to pursue this journey, but also for his inspiration—for the desire to follow and be an instrument of his will.

Looking back for a moment at my initial struggles to find sobriety, when I finally admitted I was powerless over alcohol and became willing to go to any length to stop drinking, I was offered a postulate I found difficult to accept at first. The premise was that I could regain power by admitting defeat and then turning my will and my life over to a God of my understanding. Having tried almost every other course of action to stay sober and failed, I grudgingly assented. And as I did, I heard the Twelve Step program of Alcoholics Anonymous telling me: "Lack of power, that was our dilemma. We had to find a power by which we could live, and it had to be a *Power greater than ourselves*. . . . If a mere code of morals or a better philosophy of life were sufficient to overcome alcoholism, many of us would have recovered long ago."[1]

Still, turning my will and my life over to the care of a God who I felt was stern, rigid, and unloving, a God I believed had abandoned me because of my wretched way of life, a God from whom I felt almost totally removed, was not an easy task. So I was directed to pray—to pray daily on my knees to seek a God of my understanding into whose care I could turn over my will and my life.

As my journey of recovery led me through the Twelve Steps, I came to learn more about my disease and myself. That it was not just about my drinking and drugging but also my character defects and shortcomings. My thoughts and actions changed. I began hearing more about God through the people at meetings. They spoke of his love and caring, his support and direction. Slowly my perception of my Higher Power began to evolve.

Soon I came to realize it was God who had given me this precious gift of sobriety, the power to refuse alcohol and drugs, the power to work the Twelve Steps in my life. Then came another more marvelous realization—that God was my very best friend. That he had always been there and would always be a loving friend provided I continued to seek a conscious contact with him on a daily basis.

I learned that the journey I am on has much to do with helping others, which in turn enables me to deal with life and life's problems. And as I become more aware of this, I find it easier to deal with any obstacle, since I am no longer trying to do it alone. I not only have God's power when I ask for it, but he continues to direct my life through the comments I hear at meetings, when carrying the message of recovery to others, when being of service, and when I'm practicing the Eleventh Step each morning.

Now that I have begun my Eleventh Step journey, I find that I am at peace with myself most of the time. I have already come to understand that life's conflicts and problems are all part of that journey. I know that I have been given the knowledge to understand that my Higher Power will not leave me to meet life's challenges alone. He will always give me the strength to face them, accept them, or overcome them according to his will.

Without any doubt, the greatest discovery I have already made on this spiritual pilgrimage is that the kingdom of God is deep within me. Recognizing that gives me the power to remain free from the desire to drink or drug and to build the kind of spiritual life upon which my sobriety and my life itself depend. And for that I will be forever grateful.

Prayer

Dear God, as I begin this journey each day to seek a closer conscious contact with you, my Higher Power, let me not rely on any changes that have already taken place in me, any reconstruction that you have done in my life until now. For by choosing my will over yours, all of that can be gone in a single breath. Therefore, please give me the grace to rely only on you, your will for me, your love and caring. May I continue seeking knowledge of your will and the power to carry that out, one day at a time.

Meditation

The power of God grows within me as I continue to seek God's will.

Pain, the Great Motivator

For longer than I care to remember, my drinking and drugging abandoned me to a place where I actually became accustomed to the pain in my life—the pain of unhappiness, frustration, loneliness, indigence, injured relationships, and physical problems, to name a few. I felt there was no way out. Finally, the pain became unbearable. I became willing to do anything to find a way to change that wretched existence.

In a sense, the pain gave me no choice. It was the great motivator. It led me to my Twelve Step program, where I learned I had to either surrender or die. It was a simple decision, but not an easy one, since my disease had such power over me.

I had spent so many years looking for the easier, softer way. I tried taking care of myself by staying clear of the hard tasks or difficult situations that life presented. The result was that I never grew up. I never learned how to face life and the responsibilities that come with it.

At my recovery group, I was given a set of rules for living— the Twelve Steps. I was told to mold my own actions of living around these principles as best I could. My pain gave me the desire to do what I was asked and not run from it as change became more difficult. I soon learned that the problem was within me and that the answer lay in the actions I was taking. But did I have the power to continue this journey toward sobriety?

It was suggested that I seek a Power greater than myself to help me, a God of my own understanding. Once again, the pain in my life motivated me to accept this direction. Slowly, through prayer and meditation, I began to build a relationship with a Higher Power and sense, from time to time, that Power's guidance and strength in my life.

This God of my understanding helped me at first to understand that the difficulties I had were exactly what I needed in order to seek change, to take the necessary steps to overcome those difficulties through God's great gift of sobriety. I came to realize that the only real pain and misfortune and the only real tragedy come when I suffer such torment without learning from it. So I concluded that God allowed me to reach this juncture in my life in order to seek and find some power outside of myself that could change me—change my attitude, my outlook, and my willingness to develop spiritually. At this point, God offered me the Eleventh Step.

I started each day by reaching out to God, not just to ask for relief and sympathy, but to gradually come to truly know this loving and caring God. I began to feel God's power helping me to live by the simple human values of honesty, self-respect and respect for others, and open-mindedness. It wasn't easy at first, but as my faith in God grew, so did my determination to do God's will in all things.

I found that the more I worked at my relationship with God, the more healthy and civil I became. My strength to overcome weakness, self-pity, conflict, and discord grew. What amazed me was that God never failed to answer my appeals in some way or other, and God continues to do so as long as I remain faithful in my relationship with him.

Despite my vigilance, however, I learned that old ideas don't die so easily. Mine are often rooted in the misconception of how the world is mistreating me. By seeking direction from my Higher Power and from friends in my Twelve Step fellowship, I find that the evils of the world are not what create my problems. It is my own actions that cause my own pain.

The enormous pain that once controlled my life and motivated me to try the program of Alcoholics Anonymous can, much to my chagrin, rear its ugly head at times, particularly when I am taking all the good things in my life for granted. Perhaps that is beneficial in a sense, for it helps remind me that I must remain active, vigilant, and involved and must give away what I have found in order to keep it.

However, I will be forever grateful to the Eleventh Step because, through prayer and meditation and a conscious contact with a God of my understanding, I have found there is no longer any reason to be unhappy or in pain. There is no need to be disappointed, depressed, or despairing. In fact, I have discovered that if I work this Step to the best of my ability, there is no necessity for anything other than a joyful, fruitful, meaningful, and interesting sober life—one day at a time.

Prayer

Dear God, I now understand that when pain comes into my life, it's an opportunity for me to reach out for your help and guidance. Let me thank you that my anguish led me to a life of sobriety, to a life of peace and joy I could never have envisioned. But, please, dear God, grant me the grace to reach out to you in good times as well, to express my gratitude for your many gifts, and to ask again for the opportunity to carry your message of hope and recovery to others in need.

Meditation

My difficulties in life can draw me closer to my Higher Power.

Humility Opens the Door

In launching my excursion deep into the Eleventh Step, I'm sure to find that the only roadblock standing between me and a conscious contact with my Higher Power is my inflated human ego. It is what has caused me to stumble through my life, making mistake after mistake, never satisfied because there is no possibility under heaven to satisfy the human ego. It is something I will be in contention with always.

My lack of humility colored my judgment, controlled the obsessions of my mind, and allowed my self-will to run riot. I would act like the Creator himself and then have to live with what I had created. It was all an egotistical illusion fed by my alcoholism.

I tried desperately to change my life, to find some peace and harmony. But it always had to be on my terms, my way. Finally, through enough shame, guilt, remorse, and humiliation, I came to recognize my limitations, broke through my ego, and reached out to someone else for help—another alcoholic. In the darkness of my life, when humbled by my lack of power, God touched my heart.

Through the Twelve Steps of AA, I have learned something about true humility. To be humble is to surrender, to give up trying to change people or circumstances, to give up trying to force my will upon others. Humility is being quiet, being serene and confident, knowing that God is present in every situation. That God is in charge, not me.

I have come to understand as I practice the Eleventh Step in my life that my Higher Power is not all that impressed by strength or self-sufficiency or by those who truly believe they are self-reliant. In fact, my Higher Power is drawn to people who are weak and admit it.

Over the ages, God has demonstrated how he loves to use imperfect, ordinary people like myself to do extraordinary things despite their weaknesses. The cofounders of Alcoholics Anonymous, Bill Wilson and Dr. Bob Smith, are wonderful examples of God's ways. Their work has changed the world. If God were to use only perfect people, nothing would ever get done, for there is no such thing as a flawless human being. And the fact that God uses imperfect people should buoy my spirits.

Despite all my imperfections, my Higher Power has given me a very fragile gift, the gift of sobriety. It is more precious and more awesome than I could ever have imagined; that is why I feel so humbled by and grateful for God's generosity. It is a gift my Higher Power wants me to share with others. That is why God has chosen me to be his instrument to carry the message of recovery to all those seeking a new way of life.

However, this gift given to the so-called weaklings of this world—drunkards and addicts like myself—bears with it a grave responsibility. I must be willing to carry it, to share it with anyone regardless of race, creed, or condition and at any hour of the day or night under any circumstances. I must share it willingly, with unconditional love and without judgment.

For I have come to recognize that I have little or no power of my own to influence the outcome. That power comes from God himself. That is why I must overcome my ego and, through prayer and meditation, find the humility necessary to do God's work.

So let me go forward now on my journey into the Eleventh Step with two important thoughts in mind: first, that I am God's servant, who exists to serve God to the best of my ability, and second, that I am a child of God and will be loved and valued by God always by seeking his will for me in all things.

Prayer

Dear God, help me always to be aware that I am the ideal person to carry the message of recovery because I was one of the outcasts of the world, a hopeless alcoholic. And because of my experience with such a sick and destructive life, you have made me humbly alert to the cries of distress that come from the lonely hearts of alcoholics everywhere. May I carry the message of hope and recovery with unconditional love and do your will always.

Meditation

By recognizing and admitting my imperfections, I can acquire the humility necessary to do God's work.

How to Surrender

⸺⸺⸺

During my growing-up years, I remember how I would long for the day I could do what my older siblings did, how they and their friends had the freedom to basically run their own lives and make many of their own decisions: to date, to drive, to dance—and to drink and drug. Certainly my parents tried their best to help me make the right choices, but once I hit that "magical age milestone," it seemed my self-will ran amok.

After a while, despite my own worsening circumstances, I found myself looking down my nose at "losers," finding a way to win at any cost, and sneering at the word *surrender,* regarding it as something you only did in war or at the point of a gun. So by the time I crawled into the rooms of Alcoholics Anonymous and was told I had to admit defeat, every cell left in my booze-soaked and drug-addled brain rebelled at the thought.

But I was beaten. I knew deep in my soul that I had no place left to go if I wanted another chance at life. So I turned myself over to the Twelve Steps of AA, and slowly my world began to change. But inside, the battle of self-will was still raging. I feared I might drink or drug again.

At that point I was told my only hope of obtaining the power necessary to maintain my sobriety and find some peace and serenity was to surrender myself totally and willingly to the care of a God of my understanding. However, after years of running things myself, achieving a modicum of success in my life followed by abject failure, how do I, an addict, an alcoholic, acquire the ability, the sincere desire, and the gut-level determination to surrender my will to the care of a Higher Power with whom I am only now getting acquainted?

The simple truth is, after experiencing the program of AA in my life up until now, I already know all that is necessary to surrender myself to God. I know that God loves me and wants to help me; I know that it was God who has made possible this wonderful fellowship in the first place. So while my intent is to know God better in order to draw closer to him, what I know now is all that is needed to unlock the door to surrender.

I must simply let go of all my preconceived notions of self-reliance, of all my old views and prejudices, and of my present way of doing things. I must jettison everything that can stand in the way of my finding and developing a conscious contact with God in order to unleash his power in my life, the power that can restore my sanity and strengthen my sobriety.

Because my disease of alcoholism and addiction has so dominated my life, I find that total surrender each day is no easy matter. In fact, it can be a very difficult struggle at times, but one with awesome rewards. I am already beginning to understand why I cannot afford to do everything I want to do; why the severance of an old drinking or drugging relationship, the breaking off of a business or personal relationship, the detachment from my old haunts—why things such as these are so essential to my recovery. I learn almost intuitively that such decisions bring me ease and comfort because God is not only directing me along the right path, but also assuming some of my burdens as I go.

Like many other alcoholics and addicts, I have paid a terrible price to get here. As the inner changes begin to take place, I must by my actions and commitments show my Higher Power that I am willing to walk the walk his way so that I will never have to be alone again.

I must remain forever diligent in my decision to surrender myself to God's will, for the disease of addiction is not only cunning, baffling, and powerful, it is also forever. That's why conflicts can still arise between my Higher Power and myself over what he wants me to be or do and what I think I want to be or do. I need the power that comes from prayer and meditation to stay the course and show God I am willing to do things his way as long as he continues to show me the direction.

Prayer

Dear God, because of my strong human ego, I found it difficult at first to surrender my will to your care. Perhaps it was because I knew I would have to give up the harmful actions and desires I enjoyed, the same actions and desires that fed my alcoholism. But my deepest desire today is for the peace and serenity of sobriety, and I know that comes as a result of your love for me and the power you give me to stay clean and sober when I seek and follow your will.

Meditation

My desire today is to walk the walk my Higher Power wills for me.

Surrender Brings Transformation

I cannot stay clean and sober unless I change, unless I undergo a complete personality transformation. That only comes by surrendering to a Power greater than myself.

In the past, whenever I would hear the word *surrender*, I would always think in terms of giving up, admitting defeat, walking away like some pitiful weakling or craven coward, everything that went against my bloated ego and false pride. The word for me had nothing but negative connotations, something foreign to my very nature.

Little did I realize I had often surrendered to situations and circumstances in my life mainly because past experience had shown that there would be serious consequences if I didn't. I've surrendered to a doctor's care, a pharmacist's prescription, a stoplight on a street corner, the speed limit on the highway, a policeman's handcuffs, a judge's decision.

But when it came to my drinking and drugging, it wasn't until I was beaten into submission that I even considered the idea that I was powerless to stop and might finally be ready to admit defeat. Still, when I came into the rooms of Alcoholics Anonymous and was told I had to surrender in order to find victory, my alcoholic nature shuddered at the very thought. That was because I had never experienced the true efficacy of surrender.

As the days passed, I came to realize what my disease had actually cost me. That's when I became willing to do whatever was suggested in order to get well. So I began to work AA's Twelve Steps and finally surrendered my life and my will to the care of a Higher Power I choose to call God.

The very moment I surrendered myself as completely and honestly as I could, the supernatural rush of the life of God invaded me. The dominating negative power of the world and my self-destructive desires became paralyzed, not by my act of surrender, but because my act instantly linked me to God. He assumed my burdens.

Once I surrender, God is ready to do his part as long as I am willing to do mine. My natural life and ambitions can become spiritual only by asking God for inspiration and direction in my daily life and to help me cease doing those things that get me into trouble. I must now live as though everything depended upon me and pray as though everything depended upon God.

The Eleventh Step helps remind me that I came into the program of AA totally powerless, afraid, and in a great deal of pain. It was through my fear and pain that I came to believe a Power greater than myself could restore me to sanity and sobriety. But my recovery depends completely upon my willingness to surrender.

Total surrender transforms my life. It enables me to undergo a complete metamorphosis, changing the very composition and nature of my inner self. For by surrendering my will and my life to the care of my Higher Power, I am no longer the same selfish, self-centered person I was when controlled by my alcoholism. The "bad stuff" that led to my self-loathing is replaced by the "good stuff" that was there all along but was stifled by my disease.

Through the Steps, I gradually become a mature and responsible individual with a great capacity for joy, fulfillment, and wonder. I discover the enormous potential for good that God has given me. I am no longer afraid to risk failure to develop new, hidden talents. My fears are replaced by faith.

Without surrendering myself to the care of God, I will simply be at the mercy of forces I cannot control as well as the force of my own self-will. By myself I do not have the power and inner strength to surrender my life on a daily basis without the help of God, for I am constantly being pulled in one direction or another by my character defects and shortcomings.

However, by practicing the Eleventh Step in my life each day, God will give me the insight and power to do his will, which will continue to restore my spiritual well-being.

Prayer

Thy will, not mine, be done. Dear God, please give me the insight and power to repeat those words over and over again each day so that the surrender of my life and my will to your care becomes part of my very nature. Help me to understand and enjoy the true efficacy of surrender and protect me from my old way of thinking. Please grant me the grace to walk with you each day along the road to true recovery and spirituality.

Meditation

By striving for true surrender to the will of my Higher Power, I will find the kind of spirituality necessary to sustain and expand my recovery.

Overcoming the Bondage of Self

When locked into the bondage of self, I tend to be a perfectionist in the art of self-deception. While I may act like I am being of service to others, in truth I am really seeking praise and admiration, or looking to achieve some other selfish aim.

The whole time I am setting up chairs for a meeting, for instance, or making the coffee or mopping the floor, I am thinking about how noble and generous I am. I might even try using such outwardly good actions as bargaining chips with my Higher Power: "See what a good person I am, Lord. Now you might think about giving me what I've been asking for, since I'm sure you think I've earned it."

If I would like to measure the true sincerity of my actions or how deeply I am engrossed in the bondage of self, all I have to do is look at how I react when someone takes me for granted, fails to say thank you, bosses me around, or treats me as inferior—or at how quick I am to feel anger or resentment.

Even as my active alcoholism and addiction was leading me down that dark road to self-destruction, my intellectual capacity and feelings of self-sufficiency continued to fuel my bondage of self. In other words, I remained too smart for my own good. I thought knowledge was power, that my keen intellect could conquer natural instincts run wild, and that my razor-sharp thinking could solve all my problems. As my uncontrolled drinking and drugging began to short-circuit these conceptions, I still clung to my ego-driven defenses.

Then came the fears. Yet I remained blind to what I should have feared the most—myself. For I had no power to control myself even though I thought I was in control. I was being conquered by my own self-will. The only thing that could save me was the grace of enlightenment that comes from outside oneself, that moment of clarity offered to every suffering alcoholic and addict by a loving Higher Power.

When that moment finally came for me, I let the grace of God lead me to Alcoholics Anonymous. But I entered the rooms with all the soul-sickness my disease had bred. While I was down, my defenses were still up and my bondage of self posed the strongest barrier to recovery I had to overcome.

I soon learned that my journey from that bondage to a new way of life could only be accomplished step by step. I first had to stop blaming God and other people for my problems and accept the fact that I was responsible. I had to let go of self-sufficiency and accept God-dependency. It was not an easy journey at first, especially when I was still trying to serve my Higher Power and myself at the same time. Through trial and error, pain and persistence, I finally learned that the key to my recovery was an attitude of complete reliance on God as I understand God. Once I accepted that simple yet awesome concept, my bondage of self began to slowly dissipate. It only returns when I struggle to usurp my own will for my own selfish ends.

By practicing the Eleventh Step, I realize deep within that God does indeed have the power to change my life. I simply have to pray for the strength to keep picking myself up and making a fresh start each day. I also pray for the inspiration to use the tools the program gives me and the guidance on how to best use them.

I must never forget that the final stage that comes from using the Eleventh Step is not only faith, but also the attainment of character. For God creates the spirituality I seek deep within me so that it is always there even in moments of confusion and despair. As good disciplines and habits are formed through daily prayer and meditation, I begin to discover many rewards, not the least of which is amazement at what God has done to my innermost self by working the Twelve Steps in my life.

As I continue to grow in sobriety, I discover that the moments I am truly alive are those moments when I willingly take the actions of the Eleventh Step and find they link me up with a loving God and the power he gives me to lead a spiritual life.

The bondage of self that I have lived with and its hold on me become clearer each day, as does the need to overcome it through working the Steps. I have come to recognize that the program God has given me comprises a body of living spiritual wisdom far surpassing any great intellectual capacity I once thought I had. And as I continue to study these Steps and apply them to my daily life, my knowledge, understanding, peace, wisdom, and freedom expand without limitation.

Prayer

Dear God, please remove this bondage of self so that my attitudes and motives will always match the good actions I try to take each day to honor you. Continue to guide and inspire me on this journey from the depths of my addiction to the heights of your spiritual embrace. I know now that neither my intellectual capacity nor my feelings of self-sufficiency can keep me well. My recovery depends totally on the power I receive from my growing relationship with you through the Eleventh Step.

Meditation

If I continue to examine the motives behind my thoughts, words, and actions, I will soon find freedom from the bondage of self.

A Conscious Contact with God

—————◦◦◦————

The true purpose of the AA program is to provide tools that, when used appropriately, will enable me to achieve a conscious contact with a Power greater than myself who can lead me to spiritual health and to recovery from alcoholism and drug addiction. The most important tool is prayer, for it is the pathway to that Power, a God of my understanding.

Also, as I attend AA meetings and work the Twelve Steps, I sense that God is beginning to speak to me very quietly through my thoughts and feelings and through fellow members who share with me their experience, strength, and hope.

In my search for a conscious contact, what is it I need God to provide that will sustain and bolster my recovery? Some have made these suggestions: (1) The weak need God's strength. (2) The strong need God's tenderness. (3) The tempted and fallen need God's saving grace. (4) The self-righteous need God's mercy. (5) The lonely need God as a friend.

So many times in the past I have stretched out my hands but not my heart. Now, as I draw closer to a conscious contact with my Higher Power through prayer and meditation, I learn through my actions that it is by giving that we receive—that love is extending myself for others, and by doing so I am blessed by the unconditional love of God himself.

My craving for alcohol and drugs actually constituted the low-level equivalent of a spiritual thirst—a thirst for a better life, a thirst for union with God. As I became aware of the exact nature of my problem, I became aware of my need for spiritual wholeness. At Twelve Step meetings I meet others on the same journey, and by sharing together, my spiritual thirst gradually becomes quenched.

I become filled with enthusiasm for what I have found, and I desire more. Something had to inspire this feeling, and I discover that "something" is a growing consciousness of God deep within me. I begin to put more and more trust in God, sensing that he understands my circumstances, my needs, and my desires far better than I do. In fact, I know beyond a doubt that God is offering me a new way of life far beyond my wildest dreams because he has already given me the greatest gift I have ever been given, the gift of sobriety.

The Eleventh Step and the actions it suggests open the door wider to a conscious contact with my Higher Power. I find a loving God, not the punishing God I feared before I came into the program. I realize God had been with me during all those times I had been in trouble, long before I even recognized I was in trouble.

Conscious contact simply means knowing and sensing God in my life throughout the day. I discover that prayer enhances my ability to achieve that contact. I literally see it change my life and the lives of those around me. I come to know and feel the power of God.

However, in seeking a conscious contact with God, I must be aware of the heavy responsibility I bring upon myself. When I pray for God's help, I must be willing to accept God's solution. In the past, for example, I often sought the quick and easy way out of my dilemma. This may not be God's way. That's why I cannot let any perceived urgency on my part obscure God's wise and loving answer.

Since my Higher Power led me into the fellowship to find recovery, he also wants me to seek the counsel of other members. That is often the way my Higher Power reveals himself and his solutions to my problems. In other words, when I seek God's aid, I must be receptive to the means he chooses to help and comfort me, including the loving touch of a fellow member, a good friend, a kind spiritual leader, or a wise counselor.

God has a plan for my life. It may be different from the one I envision. The key to great blessings is being willing to adjust my plan for God's will.

Prayer

I pray, dear God, that I may persistently carry out the guidance of the Eleventh Step so that I will be able to turn my natural life into a spiritual life by my obedience to your will. Please help me to be open to your way of responding to my cries for help rather than reverting to my past tendencies to find the quick and easy way out of my pain and confusion. May my conscious contact with you continue to grow as I earnestly seek to do your will.

Meditation

**How well am I using the tools of the AA program
to improve my conscious contact with God as I
understand him?**

Experiencing God's Presence

———◦◦———

As I continue seeking through prayer and meditation to improve my conscious contact with God, I can expect to be blessed by those truly awesome moments when I actually experience God's presence.

By practicing the Eleventh Step faithfully each day, I may actually feel God's presence in the varying circumstances of my life—when I nestle my baby in my arms or tuck my children into bed at night, when I caress my spouse or loved one, when I run through the mist at sunrise or walk my dog on a moonlit evening, when I take pride in a good day's work, or when I have the privilege of making a Twelve Step call on a suffering alcoholic or addict.

In these precious moments, my Higher Power is letting me know that I am no longer alone, unlike the feelings I had when being taken to another hospital or emergency room, being fired from another job, or feeling totally alone in a crowded, dingy saloon. The acute sense that there is no one who really cares, no one I can share my burdens with, is a terrifying sensation. That debilitating emotion of loneliness is no longer a part of my life, not since I began living in the presence of God. What a comfort. What a reassurance. What an encouragement. I always have a shoulder to lean on now, the broad shoulder of my Higher Power. I have someone to thank for my newfound joy. I now have someone who I know will never abandon me.

I once believed that God was remote and abstract, someone you could only find by reading the books of the ages or traveling to India or Tibet to discover him in ancient scrolls or through meditating monks. The program of Alcoholics Anonymous offers an easier path to God through twelve simple Steps.

The only thing that gets in the way is "self." When I am narrowly focused on the concerns of ego and self-will, I tend to ignore any conscious contact with my Higher Power. I become weak and confused and once more feel alone. Also, when my ego gets me to take on more than I can handle, my life becomes unmanageable again.

God does not expect more of me than I can produce. So when conscious of his presence, the challenges and difficulties I encounter are eased. God gives me the knowledge and strength to cope with them and learn from them.

As I grow in recovery, I learn to arrange my priorities so that compulsive behavior and busyness do not wear me out. Everything becomes more manageable when I'm not trying to run the show myself. Experience in the Twelve Step program teaches me that help is always at hand through my close relationship with my Higher Power.

To experience God's presence in my life, I must have the willingness to be open. I will find that God is indeed "closer than breathing and nearer to me than my hands and feet." What I may have spent years searching for, or perhaps even denying, turns out to be the ground of my very existence and the Power that sustains me every moment.

However, all of this rich, spiritual growth will only happen if I strive to stay close to my Higher Power, not just once in a while, but always. Certainly, God knows my circumstances and my needs far better than myself, but to help meet those needs and carry those burdens, God wants me to stay as close to him as he is to me. It is only by praying each day to improve my conscious contact with God that I come to know his will for me and, more important, gain the power to carry it out.

And so as I am blessed to experience the presence of God in my life, I know for certain what he wishes for me: that I continue to draw closer to him in my spiritual recovery and that I remain open to being a useful tool for him to help another suffering alcoholic or addict.

Prayer

I am grateful, dear God, for the privilege of experiencing your presence in my life and the great joy and comfort that it brings. Please help me to remain faithful to my commitment to practice the Eleventh Step each day so that my conscious contact with you continues to grow, along with my knowledge of your will and the power to carry it out.

Meditation

How has my striving for a closer relationship with my Higher Power changed my actions and my attitude about life?

God's Purpose for My Life

In this goal-oriented world we live in, how often have I asked myself, What is my purpose for being? Why did God make me? What should I be striving for? During my drinking days, each time I thought I was on the right road, my character defects and shortcomings, fueled by my alcoholic, addicted self-will, led me into another painful dead end.

Even though I've now been given this wonderful gift of sobriety, I can still be misled by my defects as I continue to seek my purpose in life. The truth is, I must be very careful not to see my particular dreams of success as God's purpose for me, because his purpose may be exactly the opposite. I must not imagine that if my Higher Power constrains me and I obey him, he will shower me with gifts and present me with some great reward.

The most important thing for me to know is that in order to stay sober, I must now live my life to fulfill God's purpose, not my own. God has chosen me, I haven't chosen him. I came into recovery a complete failure, someone of little value, and through the Twelve Steps, God is turning me into a very special person in his eyes. My Higher Power has literally given me a second chance at life.

I may have the idea that God is leading me toward a particular end. But getting to a particular end is simply a mere incident. What I call the journey, God calls the end, for he has transformed me along the way. His purpose for me is simply that I learn to depend on his power. If I use that power to stay in the middle of life and its turmoil while remaining calm and unperplexed, I have achieved what God desires for me.

The strange truth is, God is not working for a particular finish for me. His end is actually the continuation of turning me into a humble and spiritual person who can help him reach out to help others. So when I dream of God's purpose for me in life, all riches and earthly rewards pale in comparison with the truly great privilege of being of service to him.

God knows what is happening in my life each and every moment. Things do not happen or continue to happen by chance. For example, when I reflect on my so-called luck in getting to the Twelve Step program, which saved my life, it wasn't luck at all. It was the grace of God doing for me what I could not do for myself. In other words, there are no coincidences; there is no luck of the draw.

That's why I must continually practice the Eleventh Step and seek a conscious contact with a God of my understanding more and more every day. I must get into the habit of talking with my Higher Power about everything in my life. At my first waking moment, I must fling the door wide open and let him in so that today, tomorrow, and the rest of my life will be stamped with his presence.

Each morning as I pray, I should think quietly about the hours just ahead. I should ask God to direct my thinking, especially that it be free from dishonest or self-seeking motives. I ask again for inspiration and to be an instrument of his will, which

I now know is his purpose for me. Then I can relax, secure in the knowledge that all will work out because I am finally on the right road, a road that has no dead ends.

Finding sobriety in my Twelve Step program, my primary goal is to reconstruct my life. The power of God gives me that chance. And as I change through the Twelve Steps, I come to realize that the spiritual life is not a theory. It really works, but I have to live it. And when I live spiritually, God fulfills his purpose for me by providing the power that grants me a daily reprieve from my disease, as well as the strength and willingness to be a useful tool for him.

The true measure of my success at living spiritually will come not from what I do in the exceptional moments of my life but what I do during ordinary times. My worth will be revealed in my attitude toward ordinary things, not when I am before the footlights. Daily prayer and meditation strengthen my resolve to live spiritually and receive from God the openness and willingness to accept all that he has to offer. By taking these actions, I begin to understand that my primary purpose in this world is simply to help others, which is also God's purpose for me.

Prayer

I pray that I may persistently carry out my spiritual exercises every day so that I am ready and available to meet God's purpose for me in life. I pray that I may constantly strive for peace and serenity and that I will be able to transform my natural life through my obedience to him, my Higher Power.

Meditation

Do I find myself always entirely willing to accept God's purpose for me in life, or do I often continue to struggle for some reason?

Acceptance Is the Key

There was a time in my life when I thought I was the captain of my ship, the master of my fate; a time when there was nothing I couldn't surmount or solve with my own intellect and self-will. Then I crashed on the rocks of alcoholism and came to realize that I am powerless over most things in my life.

In my Twelve Step program, I have come to learn that not all problems I will face can or will be changed or eliminated. But I have also learned that in those circumstances, when I can see no immediate solution, I can find peace and serenity by accepting God's will without question.

Perhaps the greatest hindrance to achieving calmness in the midst of a storm is still my clenched-jaw resolve that I can do something about everything. That old way of thinking, which is the dregs of my sick self-will, must be suppressed. For it is only when I let go and let God that I begin to understand that acceptance is the key—that acceptance is the real answer to life and its problems. The more I work the Eleventh Step, the more direction and strength I will find and the fitter I will be for life's journey and its challenges.

I find that one of my biggest difficulties is the strain of waiting. It is during these periods that I must remain spiritually tenacious, praying for knowledge of God's will and the power not to commit an act of rebellion that could hurt me or someone else.

The Eleventh Step, however, is not a quick fix. It is my guide for spiritual living. It also exacts a price, the price of giving up my self-will. There is also the price of surrendering to become open-minded and willing to accept the need to change. Finally, the constant use of prayer and meditation provides me with the ability to maintain my faith and peace of mind.

But sometimes discouragement sets in when the answer doesn't come soon enough. I must believe that God is working on the unseen plane and that my part is to be persistent. For persistence is an expression of faith. By my persistence I am affirming my belief that God will make his answer clear when he is ready.

The most important part of acceptance is getting myself out of the way. It is God who works things out, not me. I am only the channel through which his divine action takes place. I must stop thinking about the difficulty, whatever it is, and think about God's goodness instead. If I do this, the trouble, whatever it is, will eventually disappear. It may be big or little. It may concern health, finance, a quarrel, an accident, or anything else conceivable. But when I accept it, stop thinking about it, and turn it over to my Higher Power, it never fails to work out.

There may be days when it seems like my struggles will never end—the pain, the loss, the heartache, the failures. But through prayer and perseverance I learn that all things shall pass. Given time, effort, acceptance, and patience, things work out. They may not work out the way I thought they should, but they always work out for the best.

When I think of being patient, that doesn't mean complacent. On the contrary, each new day in recovery requires a new attitude, a new outlook that in time generates its own positive energy for growth and change. I need patience and strength not only in the difficult moments, but also in the easier times as well—the days of comfort when things seem to be going almost too well. For I've learned through a great deal of pain and suffering that most alcoholics and addicts like me can't handle too much success or too much comfort unless they stay very close to their Higher Power.

There are no adequate answers to why serious problems may come into my life. And it is ludicrous to believe that every such situation involving me is by design, which is my old "blame it on God" attitude. The truth is, I bring many problems on myself—bad financial decisions, unwise relationships, angry retorts to the boss, failure to take care of important health needs. And in instances beyond my control, I have to simply trust that what comes my way is meant for the ultimate good. I may not always understand why, but experience in my Twelve Step program proves that acceptance of my Higher Power's will for me is always the best answer—and the key to my peace and serenity.

Prayer

I ask you today, my dear God, for the kind of faith that will allow me to know that no matter what happens in my life, everything will be all right because I am in your loving hands. That kind of faith will also enable me to accept whatever life brings while living with you in peace and serenity.

Meditation

Do I have difficulty at times accepting God's will in all situations?

I Must Trust God

How often I have worried about something and then, after putting myself through mental agony, finally handed the concern over to my Higher Power. The relief was stunning, almost unbelievable. Yet, almost the very next time another worry threatened my peace of mind, I seemed equally reluctant to let go and let God.

Why is that? Because I still relish the sensation of being in control, I find it difficult at times to trust someone else, even my Higher Power. I somehow feel that by pondering a problem continuously, thinking through all the options and possibilities, I will come up with good answers myself. While that may be true at times, the process saps all my energy, putting me through days, sometimes weeks, of unnecessary grief.

When I rely only on my own limited resources, I am discounting completely the wisdom and caring of a loving God. God wants me to trust him, to turn over all my perplexities, fears, worries, and impossible situations. God is the only one who can handle them, because he knows what's best for me. God has the big picture. I don't. Therefore, trying to manipulate things can only result in more confusion and concern and possibly lead me to a drink.

I must trust God and pour out my heart to him. He is always ready to listen. God will lift my burden once I turn it over to him.

In order to develop a strong trust in God, I must work the Eleventh Step each day to improve my conscious contact with him. Through that close contact and greater knowledge of his will for me will come the ability to turn things over before they reach the troubling stage.

By learning to trust my Higher Power I will also begin to trust myself, because my actions will change my thinking. I will also begin to trust others, knowing they may be part of God's way of answering my concerns.

Through prayer and meditation, I discover that the best possible source of emotional stability is my relationship with God. I learn that dependence upon his perfect justice, forgiveness, and love is healthy and that it works when nothing else does. I grow in trust to the point that I allow God to guide me on the road to sanity, the road to spiritual sobriety. I also become more aware that I am responsible for my actions and inaction, and the consequences of both.

When I express gratitude for my recovery in the Twelve Step program, I am also expressing my trust in God. For through the Twelve Steps, I have come to believe that God will never desert me and will always give me the courage to take the actions necessary to meet life's challenges.

One thing I must not forget is that sobriety is never painless. In fact, it can be more painful at times to be sober than drunk. Drinking and drugging was my escape, my way of avoiding problems and relieving pain. It took me so long to finally reach out for help, that I don't want to take the chance of ever slipping back. Yet there will be those days when it takes every ounce of trust, every ounce of faith, and most assuredly every ounce of almighty grace to take the proper action when the vision is blurred and the old self-pity has returned. By practicing the Eleventh Step, the grace and power I need for that moment will surface inside me, and I will intuitively know that God is with me to help me do the right thing.

Each and every day I stand at a turning point in my life. My thoughts and actions can either propel me toward spiritual growth or send me back down the road toward booze and drugs. I gain strength to make the right choices and accept life's responsibilities by asking God through the Eleventh Step for the power I need. Happiness and freedom in this new life will only come as a result of the effort and action I take to find and establish a trusting relationship with my Higher Power.

Prayer

In the past, my lack of trust in you, my God, has always led me down the path of pain and hopelessness. Please give me the grace to always turn to you with my concerns, problems, and anxieties, believing you are willing to lighten my burden and help me find a sobriety filled with peace and joy.

Meditation

What do I do each day to build my trust in my Higher Power?

Rigorous Honesty Frees the Soul

It is impossible to make any real spiritual progress without being rigorously honest with God, others, and myself. But that kind of honesty is only achieved through painful past experiences and the deep desire to change and live a new way of life.

Because of how I lived in the past—lying, misleading, and manipulating for any reason at all—it takes time to evolve into a truthful attitude and develop the courage to be honest on all occasions.

At the same time, alcoholics and addicts like myself who are striving to develop a spiritual way of living often make the mistake of being too hard on themselves. When I don't seem to be progressing as fast as I would like or I find myself not always being completely honest, I get discouraged and begin to condemn myself. This is foolish. If I can say I am doing my best to be truthful, then that is all God expects of me. As the AA literature states, I strive for progress, not perfection.

Therefore, I must not get impatient with myself. I should work at being rigorously honest each day, not expecting too much too quickly, but foreseeing inevitable growth and improvement.

Happiness and comfort in my recovery depend in a large part on my honesty, for I create disappointment for others as well as for myself when I am dishonest. Rigorous honesty comes from God within me and flows out to touch those around me. If I am to be a respected member of society as well as a respected member of my Twelve Step program, I cannot feel one thing in my heart and outwardly speak a different view.

There is no such thing as "being too honest." When I try to be truthful in all my affairs, I discover that the reason I should be honest is not simply because I find that it avoids problems, but that it makes my life happier and improves my self-esteem. Also, when I am honest with God, others, and myself, I am greatly improving my inner nature or character, another wonderful blessing of living a spiritual life.

As I work the Twelve Steps, I come to understand that there is a big difference between respecting my own privacy and being honest. I don't have to share every gory detail of my past with others. I can choose when and with whom I will share my private thoughts and situations, such as with my sponsor, a member of the clergy, and always with my Higher Power.

Being truthful is necessary to move forward in my spiritual life, but sharing every detail of my life with everyone—past or present, sordid or not—has nothing to do with being honest. When applying for a job or meeting new friends in a social setting, for example, I can respect my own privacy. However, with those things that still trouble me, I should share them with someone close, because ultimately the most important person I have to be honest with is myself.

The Twelve Step program tells me I am only as sick as my secrets. Dishonesty breeds fear, kills peace of mind, separates me from God, and can lead me back to a drink.

I have learned the hard way that alcoholism is a disease of denial. The Twelve Steps teach me that the remedy for denial is truthfulness. I also learn through the Eleventh Step that I am closest to my Higher Power when I am trying to be rigorously honest.

The truth never changes, because God is truth and God never changes. Spiritual growth, therefore, is the process of replacing lies with truth, the process of replacing sickness with health, and the process of changing doubt into faith. And as I continue to increase my awareness of God's active presence in my life, I will want to seek and live in the truth, for the truth will set me free.

Prayer

Dear God, you deserve nothing less from my heart than utter sincerity and complete truthfulness for saving me from the degradation of alcoholism. By putting aside my own thoughts and desires, I can better listen to, understand, and heed your will for me and can do my best to carry it out with rigorous honesty.

Meditation

What is it that blocks me from being rigorously honest with God, others, and myself in all my affairs?

Prayer Opens the Pathway to God

———————

There is only one way to make spiritual progress, and that is to continually seek a conscious contact with God through prayer and meditation.

Prayer and the rigorous use of the Eleventh Step on a daily basis will change my life. Those in a Twelve Step program who make regular use of prayer would no more do without it than they would ignore sunshine, fresh air, and food on the table. So if I go to my Higher Power in simple, affirmative prayer, it will bring peace and harmony into my life and make the feeling of well-being a reality.

I should look forward to those quiet times of communion with God when I recall the past, both good and bad, and think about who I am now and how far God has brought me. For time spent in prayer is never wasted. If I do not pray, I cannot expect to trudge very far along the pathway to my Higher Power. But if I pray faithfully and regularly and try my best to live a spiritual life, then it will only be a question of time before all trouble, all doubt, all fears, all sadness, and all mistakes fade away.

I should never hesitate to approach God in prayer just because I don't feel worthy of God's help and love. If every alcoholic and addict had to wait until he or she felt worthy, then no one would find recovery, because people cannot make themselves worthy. I must turn to God just as I am now, and however sinful and guilty I may feel, God will begin to make me worthy through his loving grace and forgiveness.

Only God can cancel mistakes and provide the power to rebuild lives. The more sense of guilt I have, the more reason there is for turning to God. The very fact that I decide to pray means that God's love has initiated my action. What greater evidence can there be of God's caring?

If I pray to grow spiritually in order to become a better person, then prayer will always work. However, if I choose not to pray because my Higher Power's answers may not be to my liking, then I will surely slide backward into my old ways.

So I should pray not to be so attached to my defects and dependencies that I am afraid of change even if such change is for the better. My biggest mistake then would be not the fear of changing, but doing absolutely nothing about it.

Through prayer, my Higher Power gives me the courage and fortitude to meet life head-on. Constant use of the Eleventh Step doesn't merely provide me with the strength to deal with my problems, it actually opens the door to their solution by creating a close harmony with God.

The trouble is, many alcoholics and addicts like myself are always looking for a shortcut, a way to build a relationship with God without taking the actions necessary. But without breathing in, one will suffocate. It is the same with prayer. It is a two-way street. People can suffocate spiritually because they breathe out but don't breathe in. For example, sometimes I'm so busy telling God what I want him to do for me that I never listen to what he wants me to do for him—or what he wants me to do for myself. The old person in me tries to get everyone else to change. The new person I am trying to be looks for ways to change myself for the better in order to help others.

By practicing the Eleventh Step, I am given the power to make my actions today part of the solution rather than part of the problem. I no longer live as a stranger in a strange land. I lose the horrible feeling of being lost, frightened, and purposeless. I now belong to God and to the human race, which belongs to him.

Prayer also enables me to discover God's will for my life, which frees me from the bondage of self and the need to drink or drug. And through that freedom I finally come to understand the grand truth—that there is no substitute for sincere, heartfelt prayer, which is the conscious dwelling on and opening up to the very being of God.

Prayer

Today I give you all of me, the good and the bad, my character defects and shortcomings, my selfishness, resentments, and dishonesty. I pray that you remove them all in accordance with your plan for me. Take me as I am and use me in your service. Please guide and direct my ways and show me what I can do for you.

Meditation

What do I find in my life more important than daily prayer to improve my relationship with my Higher Power?

Meditation Draws Me Close to God

As I advance on my spiritual journey, one of the last conceits to go is the idea that I understand myself, that I know what's good for me and what I need in life. The truth is, only God really understands me.

Conceit is one of the strongest roadblocks to a spiritual life. Perhaps that is why my Higher Power waits until I have run out of my own answers. He follows me through the crooks and crannies of my character defects until I finally see how wrong I've been, how even my best thinking can get all muddled up. Then, when I'm ready at last to hear his word and understand his directions, he begins to expound things to me as I kneel in prayerful meditation.

My Higher Power shows me the uselessness of false pride, the danger of intellectual dishonesty, and the pain of unwise relationships. As I listen, he reveals the envy and jealousy I've been blind to and the laziness and thoughtlessness I've been trying to ignore. God will open up to me in meditation all I was harboring before his grace began to change my life. And God will give me the strength to look at myself with honesty and courage.

Those who make the steadiest progress in their Twelve Step program are those who readily ask for and accept God's help. That's why the Eleventh Step should be a vital part of my life, for understanding spirituality is not an intellectual exercise but rather a case of discipline, obedience, and action. Prayer opens the channel to God, and meditation makes me able and willing to acknowledge the truth and to draw closer to him and his direction for my life. My real needs are revealed to me when I make the Eleventh Step part of my daily living.

Also, when I am alone with God, I can bring every need, dream, hurt, and longing to someone who hears, understands, and desires to take care of my every circumstance. In the quiet of my time with my Higher Power, I can listen to his encouragement, his inspiration, and his answers to my concerns. When I do all of this in prayerful meditation, my life takes on a new spiritual dimension.

I should also remember that my Higher Power is not just present with me during my morning meditation. He is with me throughout the day—at work, in the car, in the doctor's office, in the grocery store, with the family at dinner, at meetings, and at play. No matter where I go, God is always with me, for his love is ever constant.

Since God is always with me, I should make it a habit of turning to him several times each day to thank him for his strength, guidance, and inspiration. As I do this, meditation becomes a natural part of my spiritual life. I sense that my life is part of a divine plan. I become more concerned about others, less concerned about myself, and therefore less apt to head off in the wrong direction.

Through prayer and meditation I come to know with certainty that it is God alone who is my peace and comfort, my strength and courage.

Still, there will be times when I tend to forget—when life gets good and I get so busy that I neglect dropping to my knees for my daily visit with my Higher Power. At those times when I catch myself forgetting my spiritual exercises, I must stop and ask what wonderful thing is more important. In truth, there is nothing that I could possibly do with the time I devote to God each day that could bring me greater benefit, greater comfort, greater satisfaction, and greater security against my disease.

In fact, if I really have something that important and urgent to do, then getting up earlier to have time with my Higher Power through prayer and meditation will make dealing with that important thing easier and more likely to be successful. God will see that it is so.

Prayer

Without your help and guidance, my God, I am powerless and my life is unmanageable. I come to you because I believe you can restore and renew me so I can know and do your will today. Since I cannot manage my affairs and difficulties, my desires and ambitions, I place them all in your hands, knowing you will help me.

Meditation

Am I ready to accept whatever God's will is for my life?

Action, the Magic Word

All the prayer and meditation in the world will not help me unless I follow it up with action. It is the actions I take that free me from my disease; actions are what draw me closer to my Higher Power.

One of the simplest yet most important actions I can take is to step aside and allow God in, for he brings with him the great gift of sobriety and the promise of a new life.

Practicing the Eleventh Step in my life each day provides me with the strength and ability to take "right actions"—to help others, be of service, attend meetings, and work the Twelve Steps as earnestly and honestly as I can.

My character is changed for the better by the daily discipline of actions taken and duties done. If I'm having a difficult time, I should go to an extra meeting or two. If I'm feeling lonely, I should call or visit someone. If I'm tempted to drink, I should go to a safe place or be with a sober friend until the obsession passes. I must take these actions even when I don't feel like doing it. I must become responsible for my own sobriety, using God's help, or I will surely fall back into the abyss from which I came.

As I continue to grow spiritually by taking these right actions, I start to have more control over my thinking. More than any-thing else, I am able to do what is necessary to alter my attitudes.

I begin to see that I am part of everyone else, a child of God seeking answers for a sober life. I find I can stand firm, even when my knees are shaking and I want to run away. I learn to speak gently to myself even when my heart is filled with tears. I start to concentrate not so much on what needs to be changed in the world to suit me, but rather on what needs to be changed in me and my attitudes to live comfortably in the world.

By practicing the Eleventh Step, I come to realize that my illness is spiritual as well as physical and emotional. Knowing this, I am determined to build a spiritual life that can sustain my recovery one day at a time.

Through proper actions, I try to make the world around me better and happier by my presence in it. I try by my own example to help others find the way God wants them to live and try to support them along the way.

If ever I find myself unhappy in my Twelve Step program, then either I need to find a new group or I am doing something wrong. Unhappiness, frustration, loneliness, and the feeling of being oppressed or aggrieved are mental states I became accustomed to as an active alcoholic, mainly because I thought there was no way out of my terrible situation. But the action I took in joining a Twelve Step program started to change all of that. Now the actions I take working the Twelve Steps help me develop a positive and optimistic state of mind and lead me to a trusting relationship with my Higher Power, the true source of my happiness.

So if I find myself becoming unhappy and miserable again, I

have temporarily left the spiritual path I was on. I should remember that the road to recovery is not always an easy one. There can be severe bumps along the way. That's why I must hold fast to the hand of God and take the actions of prayer and meditation to experience his power and inspiration once again. I can always count on my Higher Power to pull me through any situation if I do my part.

It is only when I begin to take these serious actions to help my recovery that the real fight with my disease ensues. I am fighting all the ghosts of the past. But soon I come to recognize that by trying to turn my will and my life over to the care of my Higher Power, I sense God's help in altering my disposition and willingness to work the Steps.

The conflict is internal and is not against God. It concerns the fight to turn my natural life into a spiritual life. This is never easy. Changing my natural life into a spiritual life is only done through a series of moral choices, which are in conflict with my alcoholic past. But I have no choice except to take right actions if I wish to stay sober, happy, and serene—and the power of God is on my side.

Prayer

Please keep me ever mindful of those thoughts and actions that can harm others and myself and which separate me from your loving spirit. And when I do make those mistakes, please make me aware of them; help me to admit each one promptly and then take the necessary action to change them so that I may live in your joy and peace.

Meditation

Am I always ready and willing to take the actions necessary to continue moving forward in my spiritual life?

When I Stumble

―――→●←―――

When I awake from a terrifying nightmare, I take a deep breath and thank God that is was only a dream.

When I make a terrible mistake in life, it's reality, and no matter how much I wish I could undo it, I can't. So I castigate myself for a while over this and all the other mistakes I've made in my life that I can't change. But now that I'm in a Twelve Step program, I have a Higher Power who gives me a second chance, a third chance, and many more. The most important thing I must do in return, however, is to learn from my mistakes.

God loves me no matter how many times I stumble. But he is there to help me stumble less, if only I follow his direction and put the Twelve Steps into action in my life.

Being caught in dishonesty, anger, cheating, or blame today is not only embarrassing; it can throw me into a depression. Staying in such a state for a short time before making amends is one thing, but trying to justify my wrong actions to others or myself can only lead me into greater mistakes and more serious trouble.

Sometimes when my life isn't working out the way I would like, my old tendency of blaming others, including God, returns. I conjure up unloving parents, a corrupt society, a revengeful former spouse, and a disloyal friend—myriad real or imagined grievances I carry around in those old tapes. If only this or that were different, my life would be so much better.

Then, from somewhere deep down inside, the experienced voice of my Twelve Step program breaks through. It whispers that the only way I can be truly happy with my life is if I become willing to take responsibility for my own actions. Even when someone has actually wronged me, it is important to ask myself what role I might have played in either creating the situation or at least allowing it to occur. I must remember that as long as I hold back on forgiving others, I hold back on my own healing as well.

The use of the Eleventh Step is most vivid in my consciousness when I am in the depths of despair and all I can say is "God, help me, please." He always will when I turn to him with great needs.

I should remind myself every day how much my peace and serenity depend upon my being aware of God's influence in my life. As I face each new dawn, I should recognize my need for his guidance and never let a moment pass without making myself consciously aware of his presence and willingness to help.

I may never be free from the recurring tides of my character defects. Often it seems like one encroachment after another. I will never have a defense against these floods when they occur unless I develop a constant and continuous relationship with my Higher Power through the use of the Eleventh Step. If I come to trust and depend on him, the one who planned my life, I will find the strength to live free from these highs and lows—to live in the peace he offers me.

The roadblocks of fear, unwillingness, and lack of confidence will give way as I immerse myself in the Eleventh Step. I need help, and God will give me that help. Yes, changing to constructive habits may be slow and difficult at times, but it is always possible through the power God is so willing to give me.

Today is another new day, and it presents all the possibilities of a new beginning. As painful as my experiences with alcoholism were, I can feel stronger today because I have learned from them. Difficult times never have to be repeated. Today I can be grateful for another day with all the new opportunities it brings.

So when I stumble, I should not allow myself to stay down too long. God's love and the tools of my Twelve Step program provide me with another chance—another chance to learn and another chance to experience that God is doing for me what I cannot do for myself.

Prayer

Dear God, please forgive me for everything I have said, done, or thought this day that was not pleasing to you. Keep me safe from all danger and harm, and help me to start another new day with a new attitude, one that expresses my gratefulness to you for the many chances you have given me for a better life.

Meditation

What actions do I undertake to get back on my feet when I stumble and make another mistake?

The Need for Constant Vigilance

The price of sobriety is constant vigilance—being aware of any challenges that could threaten my recovery while at the same time being cognizant of God's power and the tools of the AA program to withstand any challenges.

The best way to remain vigilant is by practicing the Eleventh Step on a daily basis. This way, when any crisis arises, I have the confidence that my Higher Power will see me through it.

There will be times, as I try to grow spiritually, when confusion will set in. But striving to be close to God will help me through it. Vigilance is the price that a sober life demands, for it helps me form habits that transform the new me. I become open and able to accept God's direction, which makes me feel capable of doing anything I am called upon to do or face.

An important part of being vigilant is continuing to follow the Twelve Steps and doing all the things necessary to keep me away from the next drink or drug.

For example, I must continue to avoid old drinking or using companions. The seductive nature of these relationships cannot be overemphasized—the longing for the camaraderie and false sense of fellowship generated by shared addiction. As a recovering alcoholic or drug addict, I must distance myself from these and other unhealthy relationships as far as circumstances allow. Maintaining my sobriety is my number one priority, and I cannot let even the deepest of friendships or family ties stand in the way.

I must not miss my Twelve Step meetings, and, in times of stress and crisis, I should increase my attendance. Thousands of men and women have died because they stopped going to meetings and became convinced they no longer needed their Twelve Step program. My disease is cunning and is always trying to convince me that I am strong enough now to handle things on my own.

The Eleventh Step helps me to practice the slogan "Easy does it" by not trying to make up for the time I lost drinking or to solve all my problems at once. Alcoholics and others who seek quick relief, immediate forgiveness, and instant success usually drink or use again. I must avoid the temptation of instant gratification, something I once sought in the bottle. Also, particularly at the start of my sober journey, I must keep life simple by avoiding whenever possible any dramatic changes in employment, marital status, or geographic changes. I should give myself time to grow and mature spiritually before considering such important matters.

I must never take anything that can affect me from the neck up, like certain cough syrups, weight control pills, or seemingly harmless decongestants. Many leading over-the-counter remedies contain alcohol or other addictive ingredients. Many like myself have a low threshold of pain, which is one reason why we drank or used other substances—to be comfortable. Today I must be willing to let colds, headaches, and other minor illnesses run their course.

My sober life depends in a very large measure on my mental attitude and mental conduct. I may think I know this already, but if I don't remain aware of it and maintain constant vigilance, then I really don't understand it at all. I have been amazed to discover how much negative thinking I actually indulge in. The thought process is so quick and habits are so strong that unless I remain constantly on guard, I can easily fall back into my old ways and drink again.

The power that comes through the Eleventh Step builds my relationship with God. It will help keep my thinking positive. It will give me the enlightenment I need to attend meetings, work with others, and pray each day for the strength and guidance to stay sober and overcome all the worry and fear in my life. Once again my Higher Power will help me when I cannot help myself.

Prayer

I ask for the grace to be ever vigilant so that my recovery from addiction can continue to grow and my spiritual life will be strengthened. Please help me to always be aware of those things that can impede my sobriety so that I can be ready to do whatever is necessary to avoid such dangers.

Meditation

Do I now think I am able to handle things all by myself, or am I constantly vigilant?

Learning from the Past

⟡

My past can prove to be my greatest asset in recovery, but only if I use it wisely. In other words, I should only look back to learn, not regret; to be grateful for its lessons, not sorry for its pain; to contrast the miracle God is performing in my life against the horrors of addiction from which he saved me.

By practicing the Eleventh Step today, the shame and degradation of yesterday will no longer weigh heavily on my mind. It will be there only to keep my memory green. I will learn to forgive others and myself for the sins and hurts that I cannot change, only make amends for. Without forgiveness there can be no spiritual progress. Resentments, condemnation, anger, the desire to see someone else punished are things that can rot the soul. Such things will fasten my past troubles to me with rivets if I allow it.

Negative thinking from past experiences can also fetter me with many other problems that actually have nothing to do with the original grievances themselves. The more I think about my grievances and the alleged injustices I suffered, the more such trials will come to me. But the more I think of the good fortune I've had since finding recovery in my Twelve Step program, the more good fortune will come my way.

Through prayer and meditation I can rid myself of those painful experiences, many of which I brought upon myself. I tend to carry them around with me like pictures in a wallet; I am still strangely attached to such unpleasant memories.

It's my disease that wants me to hold on to past resentments, deep regrets, self-pity, and imagined hurts. It still wants me to drink over them. Also, many times I clutch these snapshots from the past because I'm afraid to feel pleasant feelings. I fear that while the Twelve Steps are working in my life today, I may not be able to cope with all the problems still in my life from yesterday. I look back and see how easily I slipped in the past and fear it could happen to me again.

But if I continue to work the Twelve Steps in my life and trust in my Higher Power, I don't have to look back with fear. I don't have to feel pain and misery any longer. I don't have to drag out that wallet and look at the images of all those unhappy times. I can fill those spaces in my wallet with pictures of joyful new moments I will want to remember.

Not letting go of the guilt from the past, about what I did or did not do, about what happened and the kind of person I became—all this can be my undoing. However, by developing a close relationship with God through the Eleventh Step, I can turn over those feelings to my Higher Power, put the past into perspective, and change who I am into what my Higher Power wants me to be.

The program of recovery that God has given to me will take the fear and concern out of looking back. I will see yesterday as a guidepost to a better tomorrow, using God's directions to light the way. A new day, a new year, a new life can be mine if I continue to walk with God. Love and friendship, support and spiritual growth are mine today. My yesterdays are over, so

I can look to the future with joyful anticipation.

Today, as a sober person, I have control over my behavior and the choices I make. I must remember to carry only the weight of twenty-four hours at a time without the extra bulk of yesterday's regrets or tomorrow's anxieties. Through daily prayer and meditation, the courage and wisdom I need will always be there.

My Higher Power has chosen to give me a new chance at life one day at a time. God wants me to live that life "in the now," not in the past or in the future. My Higher Power knows how difficult that is at first, so through the Eleventh Step, I am provided with the power and strength to meet that task—to move beyond yesterday's disaster of addiction through God's grace into the sunlight of sobriety. If I look back, I should look back with a very grateful heart.

Prayer

Let me not rue the past but instead be grateful for where it has led me, into sobriety and into your loving arms, dear God. Please give me the grace to forgive others and myself for all the wrongs and hurts that were abetted by my addiction. Help me to be grateful for these wonderful new ways of life you have given me.

Meditation

Do I still have deep regrets about my past, or have I now come to terms with it so that my past can be an asset in my life?

Examining My Motives

⟪⟫

It isn't always as important what I do as it is why I do it. That's why, in order to grow spiritually, I must continually examine my motives, particularly when those pangs of conscience deep inside start to make me feel uncomfortable.

By asking each day through the Eleventh Step to always be aware of my Higher Power's will for me, I will have a better chance to be honest with myself and not fall into the trap of self-deception.

One of the things I must avoid is exaggerating the importance and significance of my spiritual service and compliance to the principles of Alcoholics Anonymous. Even a spiritually obedient person can develop an attitude of arrogance, self-importance, and self-dependence. When I lose sight of what my real motives should be, I can find myself saying something like, "Lord, you should be proud of me. Look at all I do for you and for so many others."

That's why it's vital that I make sure my motives relate to my dependence on my Higher Power's love and generosity; otherwise I can deceive myself into believing that spiritual service will give me a special bargaining power with God and a more esteemed reputation among my peers.

Also, after people have been in the Twelve Step program for a while, there can be a tendency for them to think they know much more than the average member. I must guard against such arrogance, since it helps no one, especially me. My motive must be to continue working hard to stay clean and sober and to quietly set a good example for others simply because that is God's will for me. I cannot carry the message of recovery if my feelings of self-importance set me above or apart from my fellow recovery group members.

If I see any sign of ego-driven motives entering my new way of life, I must strive even harder to practice the Eleventh Step each day. I must ask my Higher Power to teach me the importance and efficacy of humility and to better understand that it's God's power, not mine, that keeps me sober.

Through my Twelve Step program, God offers me three things that can help keep my motives pure—fellowship, faith, and service. I learn to give without looking for anything in return. I come to understand that manipulation is a thing of the past and that openness and honesty not only strengthen my sobriety but also make me feel good about myself.

All of us want to be "somebody" at times. I can't simply deny the ego drive I have within me, can't deny that I don't enjoy plaudits and attention from those around me. However, that tendency can affect my motivations and foster within me the wrong reasons for doing the right things. To truly lead a spiritual life, my intentions must be God's intentions. My reasons for being and doing should be God's, which is why the Eleventh Step should play such an important role in my life.

Selfish and dishonest motives can only lead to trouble and ultimate failure. They will affect the way I think and act, and will create negativity in my life. I will find myself minding everyone else's business and neglecting my own. I will project the worst in every situation. I will regard my problems and difficulties as "the Lord's will" instead of accepting responsibility for them and working harder on the Twelve Steps in order to change.

Some people fool themselves into thinking that as long as they perform good deeds from time to time, their thoughts and motives are their own business. But any unspiritual thoughts and motives I allow to become habitual will sooner or later reap serious consequences. For I cannot think one way and be another. I am either real or phony, truthful or dishonest, a child of God or someone totally controlled by alcohol and drugs.

Again, it is vital that I examine my motives each day as I practice the Eleventh Step. I should pray for the power and strength to overcome all my weaknesses and defects, for they are my disease—and a spiritual life based on honesty and pure motives is the cure.

Prayer

Dear God, I ask again for your forgiveness. Help me to live this day with an attitude of gratitude. Let me make the best of each and every day, striving to do your will with pure motives so that my actions can bring you glory. Please broaden my mind and bless my heart so that I can follow your direction and change my life accordingly.

Meditation

Am I always comfortable with the motives behind my thoughts and actions and in my relationship with others in my life today?

Overcoming Fear

Before arriving on the doorstep of my Twelve Step recovery program, fear was my constant companion. It led me down the highways and byways of compulsive behavior, drove me to seek perfection to cover up my feelings of inferiority, created seething envy and jealousy over the success of others, abetted my struggles to control people and circumstances, gave me an insane urge to escape life, fueled my angry detachment from my Higher Power, and finally plummeted me into rage, isolation, and deep despair.

Fear is one of the most painful human emotions, since it is marked by alarm, terror, and constant anxiety. It wasn't until I began working on the Fourth Step of the Twelve Step program that I came to realize that fear had played a major role in my life since my earliest recollections. Although fear was always there, it was something my false pride had denied or tried to ignore. That became easier once I found alcohol and drugs. But, as my addiction began to fuel my character defects, the resultant guilt created even greater fears, fears that totally ruled my hazy universe.

Every life crisis seemed terrifying and endless. All my answers were in the bottle. Then, through the grace of God, I found my Twelve Step program. Today, having been given the wonderful gift of sobriety, I have replaced my fears with faith in my Higher Power. I now realize that every crisis is a chance for change and growth. I now have a deep feeling of hope each time I think back to past problems that seemed like mountains of hopelessness at the time.

By practicing the Eleventh Step each day, my Higher Power gives me the courage to face and overcome my fears, whatever they are. That courage is sometimes simply the willingness to wait for God's answer to my concern, to trust completely that I am safe in God's hands, and to accept the fact that while not everything is going to work out my way, it will work out according to the will of my Higher Power.

Through prayer and meditation my Higher Power gives me the strength and insight to share my fears with others whom I have now come to trust. I listen to their suggestions based on their own experiences in dealing with their own fears. When I listen to God and my fellow program members, my fears lose their power over me and I can live once again a free person.

I am striving to stop living in isolation with my problems. I no longer fear letting others know what my life was really like, since they too have lived through equally depressing experiences, many worse than mine. Seeing the great changes in the lives of those around me at my Twelve Step meetings makes me feel less fearful, and more hopeful that my life can change for the better, too.

Time spent practicing the Eleventh Step each day is never time wasted. I discover that when I am fearful or worried or tired or discouraged or in pain, my Higher Power is but a whisper away. All I need to do is ask through prayer and meditation for help and inspiration, and it will be there. If I take the action with prayerful faith, my fears will leave me, for God is always ready and willing to give me the strength to deal with the realities of life before they develop into serious concerns and turn into unreasonable fear.

The best way to combat my fear is to work at enriching my spiritual life. I can make my practice of the Eleventh Step more meaningful and fruitful by using AA and other Twelve Step literature, as well as my own religious traditions and the resources of other religions. I should remember that everyone arrives in the Twelve Step program from different highways while seeking the same destination—recovery from a deadly disease. Together we find a God of our understanding who can lead us through a new gateway to a life without alcohol and drugs.

Whenever I think about how powerless I was over the fears that destroyed much of my life, I should recall the inspirational words written long ago by an anonymous author: "Fear knocked at the door. Faith opened it. And lo, there was no one there."

Prayer

I ask today for a strong and abiding faith in you, my God, so that fear can no longer control my life as it once did. Please help me to listen to and trust others so that their experiences can also help me deal with and banish unreasonable fears from my head and my heart.

Meditation

Have the fears lessened in my life? And how do I deal with them when they arise anew?

The Blessings of a Grateful Heart

Gratitude is generally thought of by most people as an expression of thanks for a gift freely given. Actually it is much more than that, since the powerful human emotions that gratitude can stir often change one's mind, heart, and actions in unfathomable ways.

Like most people, I too may think that the experience of being grateful is primarily some kind of warm, fuzzy feeling inside, fostered by the generosity of a good friend or by an unexpected pleasant surprise. While nice feelings are all well and good, they are transient and fleeting. True gratitude should become a mind-set, a way of seeing and thinking and acting as a result of the undeserved gift bestowed upon me. It should motivate me to respond.

There could be no greater gift than the gift of sobriety—the gift of resurrection into a new life, a gift lovingly offered to me by God through the Twelve Steps. How truly grateful am I? How am I responding each day to express my gratitude?

Bill Wilson, the cofounder of Alcoholics Anonymous, always warned that sober drunks can sometimes take too much credit for their own sobriety and thus forget to remain thankful to the real source of their recovery. And he included himself in that remark. Once, during a period when Bill was totally immersed in helping to build the AA program, he said he found himself growing deaf to the voice of his Higher Power within him.

He recognized later it would have been better to feel gratitude rather than self-satisfaction—gratitude for the miracle of recovery he had so generously been given; gratitude for the privilege of serving his fellow alcoholics; and gratitude for those fraternal ties that bound him even closer to them in comradeship such as few societies of men have ever known.

In other words, as the AA cofounder points out, vision and awareness are essential to the experience of true gratitude. They create an attitude of gratitude, an attitude that opens my mind and heart to the truth of the great gift I have been given. My response should be to cherish it and share it willingly with others as my Higher Power wishes.

If I approach the Eleventh Step with such gratitude in my heart, it will greatly enhance my relationship with God and will help me to draw closer to God and to be open to all God asks of me. Certainly I can take credit for showing up and being willing to accept God's will in my life, but the greatest credit for my sobriety and second chance must rightfully be given to my Higher Power, who offered me this undeserved gift.

Again, gratitude is not simply saying thank you; it should spur me to take those actions that can improve both my human life and my spiritual life. For example:

> ☞ *I should thank God for the talents and abilities I have been given* by using them unselfishly today for the good of others.

- *I should thank God for all the opportunities I am afforded* by doing the very best I can in all circumstances.

- *I should thank God for my happiness* by striving to make others happy.

- *I should thank God for the beauty all around me* by trying to make the world more beautiful.

- *I should thank God for my health* by taking care of myself.

- *I should thank God for his inspiration* by trying to inspire others.

- *I should thank God for each new sober day* by trying to live it to the fullest.

With a grateful heart, I should use the Eleventh Step to meet my Higher Power and the world each day with a smile. I owe this to God, to the other people in my life, and even to myself, for if I walk around with a frown all the time, I will certainly not please my Higher Power, nor will I reflect the fact that my Twelve Step program is one of attraction. So I can remember to smile even if it takes a little effort some days. In truth, it will take no effort at all if I remember each day all that I have to be grateful for—sobriety and a blessed way of life.

Prayer

Dear God, how can I not be ever grateful to you for this truly unimaginable gift you have given me—the gift of a sober and useful life? Please let me never take it for granted but instead always show my gratitude by seeking your will for me in all things and asking for the power to carry it out.

Meditation

**Whenever I do take my sober life for granted,
what do I do to restore the true gratitude
I should have in my heart?**

Thinking with My Heart

————————

There is an often-used expression in Alcoholics Anonymous that goes, "It was my best thinking that got me here." This statement contains more truth than sarcasm, for the mind cannot always be counted on when it comes to honesty and sound reasoning, particularly when affected by the disease of alcoholism or drug addiction. That is why I should learn to listen to and think with my heart.

It has been said that intuition, which is really insight from the heart, is more natural for women. That may be true to some extent, but through the practice of the Eleventh Step on a daily basis, a man can learn to listen to and discern his own inner feelings and senses also. In time this becomes a God-given gift that has nothing to do with gender. It now has everything to do with my sensitivity to hear and understand things through my heart that I could never hear or understand with my head.

This realm of insight from within is the realm of wisdom, for it is where God dwells. It becomes the foundation of self-honesty as I grow in spirituality. In those quiet moments of prayer and meditation, I become able to perceive through my heart what God's will is for me and to make a firm and sincere decision to carry it out.

Bill Wilson's wife, Lois Wilson, the cofounder of Al-Anon Family Groups, was convinced that our minds can often confuse us in times of stress and difficulty, or when befuddled by our addictions. She advised in her memoirs, published shortly before her passing, that if we heed our heart and not our head, our hearts will never fail us because the heart is the center for God's love and trust. As she once shared with those in AA and Al-Anon:

> I used to believe that "thinking" was the highest function of human beings. The AA experience changed me. I now realize "loving" is our supreme function. The heart precedes the mind.

> Gazing at the sky on a bright starlit night, we are overwhelmed with wonder at the seeming limitless universe. Our finite minds cannot envision its extent and complexity, much less the possibility of other universes beyond. Likewise our finite minds sometimes question why a loving God seems to permit apparently God-loving and virtuous people to suffer the tragedies that occasionally befall them. But our hearts do not need logic. They can love and forgive and accept that which our minds cannot comprehend. Hearts understand in a way minds cannot.[2]

In other words, my thinking is not always reliable, but my heart—when close to my Higher Power—always is. For example, when I allow people to rent space in my head, they can influence my decision making. Or when problems crop up, I begin projecting, getting anxious, and spending too much time thinking about them, large or small. But when I begin focusing on what is right in my life, a sense of gratitude fills my heart and I make an immediate connection with my Higher Power. Almost instantly I feel better.

The goal for me should be to have the awareness that experiencing life on God's terms, not mine, is enough. I stop taking things for granted and seek to share my joyful heart with others.

When I try to think with my heart, I find I have a more open mind. I begin to utilize more than analyze my Twelve Step program. I have the humility that lets me know where the real power for my recovery emanates. Self-delusion leaves me. As an anonymous poet once wrote, "As a man thinketh in his heart, so is he."

The Eleventh Step helps me to draw closer to my Higher Power intuitively, with my heart more than with my head. I sense that God's power and eternal guidance are available to me whenever I ask. I pray for the gift of enthusiasm over weariness, discipline over complacency, and I pray to know, mainly during those down moments when my head is filled with meaningless busyness, that I do not have to struggle alone. God's love and strength are always with me.

The key to my survival is to stay close to my Higher Power through the Eleventh Step and to always listen to my heart because "hearts understand in a way our minds cannot."

Prayer

At the onset of fear and alarm or when trouble and stress are at hand, please help me, dear God, to think with my heart and not my head. For I know now that you speak to me through my heart and that your direction and inspiration will lead me down the path to peace and serenity.

Meditation

How can I find ways to listen more attentively to God speaking to me quietly through my prayerful heart?

A Change in Attitude

Negative thoughts can rule my life as perniciously as did my disease of addiction. In the program of Alcoholics Anonymous, it's called "stinking thinking." If that is something I suffer from, then I need a change in attitude immediately, or else I will find myself heading quickly down the path to more pain and disaster.

How often have I heard someone say—or perhaps I've even said it myself—"If I expect the worst, then I won't be disappointed" or "If I think the worst about myself, then no one else can cut me down." Such thoughts have no place in a clean and sober life.

Having been given the miracle of sobriety by God through the Twelve Step program, I am now striving to live a spiritual life, which includes doing my utmost to free my mind and heart of negative thoughts and filling my entire being with joyous optimism. The problem is, I still have many of the character defects and shortcomings that can sometimes drag me back down the road of self-pity and despair, particularly when I try to face the realities of life all by myself.

But if I hold on fast to my Twelve Step program, I will find that my Higher Power uses difficult situations to draw me closer and provide me with the strength to meet them. When my heart is broken, when I feel alone and abandoned again, when I think I'm out of options—that's when I'm most likely to turn to my Higher Power for help and comfort. It is during those times of pain and suffering that I utter my most authentic and heartfelt prayers. That's when my negative thinking begins to change and my attitude toward life becomes more optimistic. For God always gives me the hope, strength, and inspiration to continue seeking a better life.

If I refuse to take such action, then I must accept complete responsibility for my own spiritual darkness. Communicating with God through the Eleventh Step gradually eliminates self-doubt and self-disgust, the two common "cancers" that so badly ravage me. Confidence, faith, and an optimistic attitude come to me as a result of prayer and meditation. They build my self-esteem and my overall feeling of well-being.

The Twelve Steps of AA change my whole attitude toward drinking and drugging. But the Eleventh Step opens the door wide to a God of my understanding who can create within me a whole new attitude toward living spiritually. Prayer begins to take on new meaning. I become willing to listen to God's wisdom, not my own head. And I come to understand that if I do not get into the habit of taking the proper action pertaining to little things, then I will not be ready to take action when a real crisis arises in my life.

Since I lived with negative thinking during all those years of my drinking and drugging, I cannot expect it all to be gone in a few days. Old tapes take time to erase. But with the help of the Eleventh Step, I can certainly begin to imagine having a more open attitude toward God, others, and myself.

My spiritual life continues to grow as I travel the road of AA's

Twelve Step program. And as my faith in God increases, my fears subside, my hopes rise, and my attitude changes, I happily grasp the joy and pleasure God is giving me through sobriety.

Someone once said that we are all artists of our own lives. In other words, God created me, but I was given the free will to design and paint my own life's canvas. When I am thinking negatively and my attitudes are bad, my canvas will be blurred and ugly. But when I ask to use God's brush, the colors will glow and I will paint a portrait of my life that reflects the beauty God sees in me.

Prayer

Dear God, please guide and direct me today so that the portrait I paint of my life is designed according to your will for me. Help me to avoid all negative thoughts and through my faith in you have a happy and joyful attitude toward life.

Meditation

In what areas of my life do I still need an attitude adjustment?

Keeping My Sidewalk Clean

Among the more meaningful expressions in the program of Alcoholics Anonymous is the one that strongly advises me to clean up my side of the street and keep it clean. In order to do that, I must carefully examine my role in any wrong or hurtful life situation and take positive action to make my part in it right.

Taking the daily inventory suggested in the Tenth Step can foster wise conduct and a pure heart. Then, as I approach my Higher Power through the Eleventh Step, my character defects and shortcomings have less of a chance to interfere with my improving relationship with God. I become more open to my Higher Power's guidance as to what is best for me right now—not what is easiest or most comfortable, but what is truly best for me.

By taking my personal inventory on a regular basis, I will be aware of any warning signs that can threaten my spiritual life and lead me back to a drink or drug. Some of the warning signs may include easing up on the practice of rigorous honesty and humility, becoming cocky over my success in my Twelve Step program, allowing complacency to lower my defenses, losing interest in new members by not making the time to help them, forgetting that alcoholism and drug addiction are deadly diseases, and no longer studying the Big Book of Alcoholics Anonymous and other recovery literature.

The antidote for these dangerous attitudes is simply to reverse course, to redouble my efforts in the program, to recognize all that I have to be grateful for, to admit my mistakes, and to once again turn my will and my life over to the care of my Higher Power.

A daily review of my weaknesses as well as my strengths will help me not only to discern the future but also to live fully in the present. With sobriety, my days become busier, filled with more activities with friends, family, job, and meetings. A daily review helps me to do things because I *enjoy* them, rather than because I think I *should*. This can help prevent future discontentment and resentments. Recovery doesn't mean loading myself down with more and more things to do. It means enjoying what I do while still meeting life's responsibilities.

While taking stock of my strengths and weaknesses, I must not be too hard on myself. Focusing only on my defects can be discouraging. I must also recognize the positive attributes God has given me, which I can now use to help others. As the Greek philosopher Socrates said: "Know thyself." Know your strengths and weaknesses, your relationship to the universe, your spiritual heritage, your potential, your aims and purposes. Take stock of yourself.

The Twelve Steps of AA teach me how to love and respect myself, forgive myself, trust myself, and have the right attitude toward others and myself. The Steps help me to reconstruct myself into the kind of person my Higher Power can be pleased with, the kind of person I can be happy to live with the rest of my life.

Before retiring at night, I should ask myself two things: First, for what moment today am I most grateful? And second, for what moment today am I least grateful? Then I should make peace with God and myself and prepare to make amends if I have harmed someone that day. Upon rising, I will be ready to greet God once again through the Eleventh Step with a clear conscience. There will be nothing standing in the way of my conscious contact with my Higher Power, who will provide me with direction and inspiration.

My "spiritual leakage" always comes not so much from troubles living day to day but from my imagination and perception of those troubles. By keeping my side of the street clean, I can remove those troubles from my mind.

The Eleventh Step allows me to maintain my concentration on doing the next right thing in my daily life. As I grow spiritually, I try to repay God and my Twelve Step program for the tremendous gifts and benefits I have received. The best way I can repay that debt is by living a spiritual life and helping others find what has been so freely given to me—sobriety.

Prayer

I thank you, my God, for everything in my life. I pray that you will keep me honest with myself so that I can be honest with you and others. Please help me to be aware of anything that could cause me to regress, and if I do, please give me the strength and inspiration to make everything right again.

Meditation

How clean is my sidewalk, and what do I do each day to make sure it stays that way?

Keeping an Open Mind

Spiritual growth helps me to understand that no one is perfect—that all of us struggle with similar demons, share similar fears and sorrows, and seek to do the best we can with what we have.

By practicing the Eleventh Step on a daily basis, I learn to accept myself with all my weaknesses, flaws, and failings. In so doing, I can begin to fulfill an even greater responsibility: accepting the weaknesses and limitations of those I love and respect. Then and only then does it become possible for me to accept the weaknesses, defects, and shortcomings of those I find difficult to love.

If I strive to keep an open mind, my Higher Power will give me the tolerance not to set myself up in judgment of others but to understand that, like myself, everyone has a right to be wrong.

The disposition to tolerate beliefs and practices differing from my own is an important part of the personality change that the Twelve Steps help me undergo. Keeping an open mind is a good sign of growing emotional maturity.

Intolerance, on the other hand, breeds spiritual illness. It is that part of my addictive personality that I must try to change by asking my Higher Power for the insight and humility to appreciate and love all creation. By checking this character defect each day as I pray to God in the Eleventh Step, I can determine just what sort of progress I am making. A closed mind is one of the fastest roads back to my addiction.

Keeping an open mind helps me to see my own life more clearly and appreciate all of the ordinary things I have around me—my family and friends, a good meal, a warm place to sleep, the ability to work again. There was a time when the sun rose and set, the seasons came and went, and I took it all for granted. Today I can recognize how beautiful and striking the ordinary things can be, and I am grateful for it.

In the past, when my mind was often shut tight or muddled by my addiction, I never knew how to utilize my talents or achieve my dreams. I was cut off from awareness by my inner struggles. My Twelve Step program opened my eyes and my mind to the possibilities of a sober life in which I could dream again and use the talents God has given me to make my dreams come true.

Today my awareness, bolstered by my sincere practice of the Eleventh Step, awakens me to the eternal miracle of life and its limitless possibilities. I can see that by helping others I please my Higher Power and help myself. I now enjoy beauty everywhere—from a pretty flower to a cool mountain stream, from a lovely sonnet to a great classical symphony. By seeking God's direction, I can avoid all the blind and ugly spots when considering my problems today.

Tolerance fuels my spiritual growth and brings many blessings. I find myself becoming less selfish and more generous. Rather than being anxious over whether I will have enough, I become more open-hearted with others. Where I see a need, I help out. When I am hurt, I become more forgiving, knowing how many times I've hurt others. I learn to receive gifts with humility and respect.

As I continue to grow spiritually, I become aware of all the walls I built in the past. They closed me off from God, as well as from people and ideas that could have helped.

In recovery I have found people who are not so fixed in their thinking. They don't pass judgment or criticize quickly. Their tranquility is obvious and infectious. Their openness allows them to hear more from others, which is the way to knowledge, change, and growth. I now know it is a blessing to share their experience, strength, and hope.

As I become more open-minded myself, I realize my Higher Power is offering me a new understanding of fellowship and love. It is building a bridge between my heart and God's heart, one that leads to a truly spiritual and sober life.

Prayer

Dear God, I recognize today that my closed mind led me to be intolerant of others and even at times to be intolerant of you. Please forgive me for my past and open my mind and heart so that I can better learn to love you and all of your creation.

Meditation

What actions do I take each day to remain open-minded and tolerant?

Patience and Persistence

————————

There are days when it seems as though my struggles, past and present, never end—the pain, the disappointments, the anxieties and fear, the heartaches. I can recount them over and over as though they never go away. But they do.

An old-timer in Alcoholics Anonymous, trying to calm a newcomer one day, asked if the person had ever read the Bible. "A long time ago," replied the newcomer. "Well, if you will read it again," the old-timer smiled, "you will notice that it always says, 'And it came to pass.' It never says, 'And it came to stay.'"

That's why I should begin each new day by acknowledging that all things do pass, that given time, effort, patience, and persistence, new things replace the old. I learn to accept or handle whatever comes along.

But patience doesn't mean being complacent. On the contrary. It means, in the case of my Twelve Step program, that recovery takes time and that new attitudes can generate positive energy for growth and change.

The daily practice of the Eleventh Step can help me acquire patience and persistence, for these virtues have to be developed slowly through a consistent effort. By committing myself to prayer and meditation, my Higher Power will give me the restraint to remain calm and hopeful during trying times. I will begin to see how much my growing relationship with a God of my understanding changes my negative thoughts into positive ones and imbues me with optimism.

I must never let myself think that I cannot do something useful with my life or accomplish great goals. Yes, I was a failure in the past, but now with my Higher Power's great gift of sobriety, I am being regenerated by the Twelve Steps. This will give me the strength and ability to accomplish whatever is God's will for me.

There may be times when that supply of strength or the answers I seek will not be immediately available because I am not yet ready to receive them. Also, some days the willingness to do what is necessary requires more prayers. But as I take the actions suggested in the Eleventh Step, the strength and answers will surely come.

The truth is, God will always answer my prayers. As I've often heard, sometimes the answer is simply no, and at other times it's "Be patient." The Eleventh Step can help me develop a faith and trust in my Higher Power that will not only help me stay clean and sober, but will also direct every area of my life if I am willing. It used to be that every time something went wrong, I would run away. Now I only think about running. While it may take time for the running feeling to pass, I know it will if I continue to work the Twelve Step program to the best of my ability.

Do I still harbor somewhere in the back of my mind the idea that I'll never really be able to change my bad habits, that my old way of thinking will never totally pass? This kind of thinking can be a serious roadblock to recovery. Part of the reason

I may still think this way is that I want to change things too quickly. I must work at being patient with myself while asking God to help me work the Twelve Step program with more persistence. I must learn to "give time time" and be patient, while still taking the action necessary to stay clean and sober.

By practicing patience and persistence in my life, I will learn to bend with the stresses and strains, like a tree bending in a storm. Seeking a conscious contact with my Higher Power through the Eleventh Step will help me develop the resiliency of spirit to spring erect after the storm has passed. With God I will find peace, quietness, and tranquility—an inner serenity that, even in the midst of whirling activity, will keep me from losing my poise.

With patience, I will take the time to pray and meditate, seeing it not as a daily burden but as a daily joy, a time to commune with and draw closer to my Higher Power, who has given me this chance to live anew. God will teach me how to accept life as it comes, understanding that all things pass away, but with sobriety, the best is yet to come.

Prayer

You are the eternal God, and in eternity there is no time, no rush, no strain. Please help me to understand that I am already living in eternity, since life in the hereafter is simply a continuation of the now. Therefore I should not be in such a hurry to make up for lost time, since time learning your will for me is not wasted. Teach me how to live comfortably in the now and to be patient with myself as I strive to follow your direction and grow in recovery.

Meditation

The virtues of patience and persistence are not easy to acquire. What am I doing each day to develop them in my life?

Happy, Joyful, and Free

How often have I heard the words *happy, joyful,* and *free* rever-berate around Twelve Step meeting rooms? It seemed as though they were mine for the asking—the door prize given free of charge to every alcoholic or addict who qualifies for a Twelve Step recovery program. Of course, nothing could be further from the truth. While they are three simple words, they are also hard-earned, precious commodities.

Some people go to the movies, amusement parks, the circus, or away on expensive vacations in order to find happiness. They seek it in relationships, sex, money, power, and success, only to discover that these often brief outside stabs at happi-ness are fleeting. For, as I've heard constantly at Twelve Step meetings, "Happiness is an inside job."

It's through the Twelve Steps of the program that I remove the negativity of my past and undergo the necessary spiritual changes that can open the door to meaningful joy. Then as I practice the Eleventh Step on a daily basis, I build a strong relationship with my Higher Power, the true source of happi-ness, joy, and freedom.

Through prayer and meditation, God will help me overcome self-pity, sorrow, pain, discord, and conflict and show me how to raise the quality of my thoughts, words, and actions. This will greatly lift my self-esteem and renew my self-respect.

As I grow spiritually, my whole perspective on life will change. I will begin to dream again, have reasons for getting out of bed in the morning, and feel a glow inside that comes from achieving positive things in life. I will be accomplishing the three essentials for happiness in this life: something to do, something to love, and something to hope for.

I may have had serious difficulties in the past exacerbated by my addiction—lost jobs, severed relationships, financial and legal difficulties. But I don't have to live out that script for the rest of my life.

The trouble is, I often think happiness consists of the fulfillment of my wants and desires or, at the very least, the freedom from pain and suffering. Actually, real happiness consists in the serenity that comes from conforming my will to the will of God, as the Eleventh Step teaches. I achieve happiness by preparing myself to accept what God wants me to do.

When I think about the people I most enjoy being with, they are usually happy people who are comfortable with themselves. That's because being happy, joyful, and free is almost the entire secret of being likable. It's infectious.

Being happy is rooted in self-acceptance, in feeling loved and wanted, and in being of service to others. That's why I can experience no greater happiness and joy than the feelings that come from helping other suffering alcoholics and addicts, bringing them to Twelve Step meetings, becoming their sponsor, and watching them change and recover. The reason is simple: I am doing God's work and have the true source of joy at my side.

While it may seem contradictory, even people with heavy burdens and great personal sorrow can find underlying happiness through the Twelve Steps and faith in a Higher Power. In other words, I can be happy today in spite of things that others would consider burdensome and depressing because I have come to understand that happiness, joy, and freedom emanate from the loving God inside me, not from anything outside of myself.

Alcoholics and addicts like me were restless, irritable, and discontent. I sought pleasure in overactivity, a wild self-will, and uncontrolled drinking and drugging. My mood swings were erratic and I could not be still. I never found any peace, inside or outside of myself.

Practice of the Eleventh Step helps me find the peace I once sought. I now find it through prayer and meditation. I learn how to relax in my Higher Power's presence, listening to the direction and inspiration of a God of my own understanding. As I continue to grow in my spiritual life, I will become free of the past and free from discontentment, and I will find true happiness in the arms of my Creator.

Prayer

God, I thank you for the promise of this new day. I begin it aware of your presence and pray it may be a day of spiritual growth and service to you. Please keep me aware of the true source of happiness, joy, and freedom, for I know this is what you want for me as I walk the road of recovery from alcohol and other drugs.

Meditation

Am I still seeking happiness from the outside, or am I now taking the actions necessary to develop inner joy?

Peace and Serenity

———⟨※⟩———

Dr. Robert Smith, the cofounder of Alcoholics Anonymous, once said, "If alcoholics are contented only when getting what they want, they're going to be disappointed most of the time."

Since I can't get everything I want in life, the best way to have peace and serenity is to learn how to enjoy what I have. And the best way to do that is to take a regular inventory of all the God-given blessings I have in my life today, putting at the top of the list the gift of sobriety.

One of the surest ways of bringing more peace and serenity into my life is by working with newcomers in my fellowship. By sharing my experience, strength, and hope, I will be reminded in a very dramatic way of all I have been given by my Higher Power through working a Twelve Step program. I will see clearly how much pain, fear, and despair have been removed and replaced to a large degree by an inner calm and peace.

The daily practice of the Eleventh Step adds much to that inner calmness. Through my Higher Power, I learn to enjoy all those things I usually take for granted, such as the simple fact that I can breathe, see, hear, smell, and sense all the beauty around me. I can walk, talk, cuddle a child, and spend time with those I love who also love me.

I no longer need to be alone or lonely. I can work, pay my bills, and take care of my health. I can enjoy a variety of interests, from sports to family gatherings. And most important, I can be available each day for God to use as a helpful tool—to do my Higher Power's bidding, whether it be to help another suffering alcoholic or anyone else in need.

When I kneel each day in prayer and meditation on the Eleventh Step, I am filled with peace and serenity as I recognize all of the wondrous gifts my Higher Power has already bestowed on me through sobriety. God also makes me aware that in my weakness lies my strength, that by admitting my powerlessness God gives me the power and inspiration to walk the spiritual path of recovery.

The well-known clergyman and spiritual writer Emmet Fox once noted this truth: "I cannot enjoy peace and serenity if I also entertain opposing forces in my life. I cannot have harmony if I enjoy gossip and criticism; I cannot benefit from the efficacy of prayer if I hold on to resentments; I cannot have a sense of divine love if I hold on to my fears and anxieties; I cannot have peace of mind if I'm not trying sincerely to do God's will; and I cannot have a feeling of toleration and understanding if I am unwilling to forgive."

The Eleventh Step is a means by which I can generate a whole new way of perceiving things and regenerate my soul to experience it anew. It doesn't mean simply improving my old self. It means knowing a new self through the power of God.

If I do this, everything else in my life will change for the better. Not only will I find inner peace and serenity, but my whole self will radiate peace. Others who are also seeking peace and serenity will be attracted to what I have found, and I will share it willingly with them. But I cannot radiate such peace unless I possess it, and I can possess it by developing a close personal relationship with my Higher Power through the Eleventh Step.

In that regard, I may sometimes be inclined to think that the time I spend on my knees each morning in prayer and meditation is the only thing that counts. That's not so. The mental attitude I maintain throughout the day is every bit as important. If I place myself in God's hands in the morning and then, throughout the day, hold myself open to do my Higher Power's bidding, I will surely enjoy the kind of peace and serenity that will radiate all around me.

Prayer

I ask you today, dear God, to direct all my thoughts, words, and actions, together with my will and my life. Help me to do all my daily tasks willingly and well, and to be aware of all opportunities to help others as you have helped me—and to share with them the peace and serenity I have found through you in the Twelve Step program.

Meditation

What are those things in my life today that can lead to my discontent, and what am I doing to rid myself of them?

Belief and Faith

⎯⎯⎯⎯⎯

When I find I am trusting more in myself than I am in my Higher Power, I must recognize this as a danger signal—that I may be on a path of spiritual decline, one that could lead to a physical, mental, and spiritual relapse. For I have now taken control again of my own destiny.

This problem often arises when things are going absolutely great. I think I'm back in control and, without realizing it, I've taken back my own will. But then comes a setback—illness, a troubled relationship, or serious financial problems. With an attitude of self-reliance, how long will I spend trying to save a sinking ship before calling upon my Higher Power to help me? Will my prideful self be able to let go once more and turn things over to God?

This is why I must practice the Eleventh Step each and every day so that I maintain a trusting relationship with a God of my understanding, sustained by a strong and abiding faith that keeps me moored in a safe harbor when being assaulted by the storms of life.

To begin with, I must recognize that there is a big difference between believing there is a God and having faith to turn my will and my life over to a Higher Power who will guide and direct me and meet all my needs. I can gain insight from two old and well-known stories that illustrate so dramatically the difference between belief and faith.

The first is about one of the world's greatest acrobats, a tightrope walker who came one day to challenge the mighty power of Niagara Falls. Thousands gathered to watch him walk across the roaring waters on a thin cable stretched above the falls. It was a breezy, misty morning as he jumped up on the cable with his balancing pole in his hands, turned to a man in the crowd, and asked, "Do you believe I can walk across Niagara Falls on this tightrope?" The man replied, "Of course. You're the greatest tightrope walker in the whole world." The famous acrobat smiled and said, "Then get on my shoulders." The man politely backed away, saying, "No, I don't think so." Yes, he believed in the acrobat's great reputation, but he didn't have enough faith in his skill.

The second is about a woman who edged too close to the top of a thousand-foot cliff and fell off. Halfway down she managed somehow to grab onto a small branch protruding from the side of the cliff. Dangling there five hundred feet from the bottom, she screamed out: "Is there someone up there? Please help me!" Suddenly a gentle voice from the clouds overhead replied: "Yes, I am here and I will help you. Just let go, my dear. Just let go." After a few moments, the woman screamed out again, "Is there anyone else up there?"

The Twelve Step program suggests that I surrender myself completely to the care of my Higher Power. It is only when I become totally willing to rid myself of "self" that I sense God within me and trust becomes almost automatic. I find myself grateful for the peace and well-being that follows. Practice of the Eleventh Step becomes easier because I now understand that prayer and meditation are the powerful weapons I need to free me from the ego and bondage of self.

Choosing dependence on God does not take away or limit my personal freedom at all. It does, in fact, enhance it, since it is I who must choose to be dependent upon God's will. It is I who freely choose to turn my will and my life over to my Higher Power each day. By taking the actions of the Eleventh Step and those Steps leading up to it, I will in time create my own very special relationship with my Higher Power. It will blossom into a deep faith based on these actions—the kind of faith that will enable me to know that no matter what happens, everything will be okay because I am in God's hands.

Right actions, particularly the action of prayer, build a foundation for a strong faith. As Abraham Lincoln once said, "I have been driven many times to my knees by the overwhelming conviction that I had nowhere else to go."

I should be aware that the final stage of using the Eleventh Step is not only the attainment of faith, but also the attainment of character. Right actions also form good habits and instill self-discipline. I will be amazed at the changes God is making within me as my faith grows and I continue to work the Twelve Steps of recovery in my life.

Prayer

God, I give you every fear, uncertainty, and difficulty I face, together with every success and good thing I achieve. I have faith that you will provide the strength, grace, and perspective I need to do your will in all situations in my life.

Meditation

What actions am I taking today to increase my faith in my Higher Power?

Spirituality and Religion

⸺⸻⸺

There are many ways to describe the difference between spirituality and religion, but perhaps the simplest is this: Religion is our attempt to show how much we love God, and spirituality is our attempt to become humble enough to allow our Higher Power to show us how much we are loved.

Knowing how much God loves me will help me achieve the ultimate goal of my journey to be free from alcohol and drugs—the goal of living on a spiritual plane. Certainly no one, including myself, can ever hope to make this journey in a perfect manner. I am not a saint. But doing nothing is no longer an option.

In order to stay clean and sober, I must begin taking the actions necessary to walk the spiritual path of life. As I make the attempt, I will find the inner strength along the way being supplied by a loving Higher Power

The Twelve Step program of Alcoholics Anonymous teaches me that I am suffering from a deadly and incurable illness that requires a spiritual solution. It tells me that lack of power is my dilemma and in order to recover from my addiction I have to turn my will and my life over to a Power greater than myself. So I ask, Where do I find that Power?

Some who come to the Twelve Steps believe at first that they are either agnostics or atheists. Others arrive as fallen-away practitioners of a particular religious faith or denomination. When some first hear the word *God* mentioned at an AA or other Twelve Step meeting, it often shakes them to the very core of their prejudices and disbelief. But for those of us who have reached the point of utter despair, there is nothing else to do but stay and listen to the fellowship's message of hope and recovery.

The first thing many of us heard that helped lower our guards and soften our sick egos was the suggestion that we could choose a Higher Power of our own understanding, be it a sponsor or simply our Twelve Step group itself. We were not bound to select a God that was preached by any particular brand of religion with dogmatic precepts we had to follow. As a result, the "God thing" was easier to swallow.

I've also learned that while AA itself is not a religion in any shape, manner, or form, neither does it criticize or speak against any religious faith or organized religious movement. In fact, the Twelve Step program actually encourages such participation for those who find that religion can enhance their spiritual growth.

As my life goes on and my sober journey continues, I become more and more aware that a spiritual way of living can only be achieved by taking the right actions, by doing things that are contrary to my ego, since true spirituality is a by-product of becoming humble. When I understand this, I am ready to accept the Third Step prayer:

> God, I offer myself to Thee—to build with me and to do with me as Thou wilt. Relieve me of the bondage of self,

that I may better do Thy will. Take away my difficulties, that victory over them may bear witness to those I would help of Thy Power, Thy Love, and Thy Way of life. May I do Thy will always![3]

This prayer helps me to realize that I was truly in bondage—to my disease and to my self-will. I begin to understand just what that means and how it can still affect my life. As God began to relieve me of the bondage to my addiction, I became better able to do the will of my Higher Power. As a result, my inner conflicts grew fewer. I became better able to believe that there can be a God who truly loves me and is always there to bolster my recovery.

I also have come to realize through the daily practice of the Eleventh Step that God did not help me get sober so that I could have a free ride. My Higher Power did not intend for me to seek a lifestyle that would allow me to continue searching for the easier, softer way. God gave me the gift of sobriety and many other gifts to help others. That is my clear pathway to spirituality—being a sober, useful person who can be called upon to do the will of my Higher Power in all things.

In truth then, a successful life is simply one that is on a journey toward a spiritual goal—to live on a spiritual plane. I don't know when or if I'll reach that goal, but it is the striving for it that makes it all worthwhile. In the eyes of my Higher Power, a winner is simply a loser who keeps on trying.

Prayer

Dear God, please help me to try today to show you my love. Give me the grace to be humble enough to understand how much you love me. I pray that I may draw closer to your love each day through my practice of the Eleventh Step.

Meditation

Let me set aside some time each day to meditate on the Third Step to understand why I should turn my will and my life over to the care of God.

Change from Within

———⊰●⊱———

How often I have fallen prey to that typical alcoholic trait of complaining. It is one of those serious character defects that can only be changed from within, for it feeds on and grows out of feelings of discontent.

While certainly more prevalent during my drinking days, those times when nothing is to my liking can still occur in sobriety. My neighbors are difficult people, my fellow workers are unfriendly, and even my family and friends don't understand me.

The best therapy for relieving this inner discontent is working harder on the Eleventh Step by spending more time in prayer and meditation. As I ask my Higher Power for greater self-honesty, I will recognize the true miracle I've been given, which will make me more grateful and more content.

Instead of constantly complaining, I will come to regard even unpleasant experiences as opportunities for growth. For example, when I pray for patience, God may put me with those who tax me to the limit. When I pray for peace and relaxation, my Higher Power may give me chances to do things for others. When I pray for love, God may surround me with unloving people who will test my nerves and hurt my feelings. And when I pray sincerely to do God's will, my Higher Power may help strengthen my spiritual life by giving me the opportunity to turn stumbling blocks into stepping-stones. My faith grows stronger the more it's tested.

By practicing the Eleventh Step each day, I come to realize that my Higher Power is involved in the minute details of my life every day. God is constantly guiding my actions to strengthen my sobriety and improve my spiritual way of living. So even when I complain and express my discontent, I must remember that my Higher Power accepts me just as I am right now.

When I look at the past, the gravity of my problems with alcohol and drugs are self-evident. My addiction affected my habits, my moods, and my misconceptions over a period of years. It sparked irrational thoughts and actions that made my defects and shortcomings flourish within me. The Twelve Steps of Alcoholics Anonymous are enabling me to undergo a complete change, a marvelous regeneration. They help clear away the debris so that I can have a close relationship with God, who is within me.

The Eleventh Step tells me exactly how to stay in regular contact with my Higher Power—through daily prayer and meditation. That is how I come to know God's will for me, become submissive to it, and find great contentment in my life. I begin to sense my disposition being altered, my ears unplugged, and my mind opened. I come to understand that I can endure any discomfort or pain with God's help, knowing that nothing lasts forever. Everything passes in time.

One of the most important things my Higher Power has given me through the Twelve Step program, in addition to freedom from alcohol and drugs, is the ability to take "right actions."

As I continue to take these actions by working the Steps in all my affairs, I come to find a life beyond my wildest dreams.

The removal of shame, guilt, remorse, and denial from my life has changed me from within. I now have the desire to seek a deeper relationship with my Higher Power, who made all this possible. I want to attune the rest of my life to this enormous source of power, and the daily practice of the Eleventh Step will enable me to do just that.

There is only one method of true spiritual progress, and that is the practice of the presence of God. Like many alcoholics and addicts, I often seek a shortcut, because the disease of alcoholism and drug addiction tends to make me lazy and sometimes unwilling to do the work necessary to achieve a spiritual goal. The grand truth is that there is no other way but through daily prayer and meditation.

If I really want "contented sobriety," I can find it by seeking the answer to this simple question: "What does God want me to be and do?" The answer is also simple. God wants me to be the very best *me* I can be—the best parent, the best sibling, the best grandparent, the best friend. In other words, God offers me contentment within by concentrating on serving others rather than always serving myself.

Prayer

God, help me to recognize and cooperate each day with your will for me so that I can continue to change from within. Inspire me with quiet confidence and courage to take the right actions that will draw me closer to you and enable me to find peace and harmony in your presence.

Meditation

What do I have to complain about today, and what changes am I trying to make within me to resolve them?

Eternity Is Now

How often do I think that dying is the end of life—a life that has to be struggled through courageously in order to earn the rewards of the next life?

The truth is, there is no "next life." I am already in it if I believe and have faith that God is already within me. That's why I should continue to enjoy my sober existence, striving to do and be the best I can, because eternity is now.

Certainly things will change once I cross the threshold from a natural, physical life to a purely spiritual life. But if I am striving to live a good spiritual life now, much will be the same. There have been all kinds of predictions and prophecies, along with the sharing of near-death experiences, that paint a variety of pictures of what the spirit life may be like. But since God is constant, the relationship I build with my Higher Power through the Eleventh Step will never change, even when my days are no more and forever continues on.

Some theologians describe heaven as a place where I will be transported into the presence of God; they picture heaven as filled with peace, love, and joy, a place completely absent of tears, heartache, tragedy, disease, and suffering. They say it is a place where I will be spiritually regenerated.

But if eternity is now and I try to live the Twelve Steps to the best of my ability, then why can't I have heaven on earth? The peace, love, and joy I find in the program doesn't ever have to end. And if I practice these principles in all my affairs on a daily basis and continue to seek a closer, more personal relationship with my Higher Power through the Eleventh Step, I will become spiritually regenerated right here on earth.

My responsibility, now that I have turned my will and my life over to the care of God, is to live each day as though it were my last one here on earth, as though I were about to cross the threshold into the life of the spirit. Have I done all I could do to make myself presentable to meet my God face to face? Since I was given the precious gift of sobriety, have I always been ready and willing to do God's bidding, to help others as I have been helped? Have I always tried to love others the way my Higher Power loves me?

While eternity is now, thinking about the possibilities that may lie before me when I cross the threshold into the life of the spirit can be comforting, even enjoyable. For if my experiences with a loving God through the Eleventh Step are pleasing and fulfilling now, I can imagine the sheer ecstasy and rapturous joy of being in God's home and enjoying in far greater measure the kind of life my Higher Power has already shown me is possible.

I can picture myself at last ending my earthly struggle, laying down my burdens and disappointments, kicking off my painful shoes, and filling myself with the joy of the eternal day. And yet, if I live the Twelve Steps to the best of my ability, I can know a measure of that peace and solace in the eternal now.

Whatever happens when I cross the great divide, I will be taking with me all that I have done to build my character, not all that I have done to build my career and earthly fortune. There is an old fable that seems quite apropos on this subject:

> There once was an ancient king who had a foolish servant whom he loved dearly. One day the king gave his servant the gift of a golden bell, saying, "If you should ever find a greater fool than you, place this golden bell in his hands." Many years later, as the king lay dying, he called for his foolish servant, telling him: "I am so ill-prepared for my spiritual journey. I have been so busy on matters of this world that I have done little to prepare for the next." The foolish servant, with tears in his eyes, placed the golden bell back into the hands of the dying king.

The Twelve Step program of Alcoholics Anonymous does not claim to have all the answers when it comes to spiritual matters, any more than it claims to have all the answers when it comes to alcoholism and drug addiction. But through the experience of the many sober miracles who have preceded me into the fellowship, I can rest assured that if I follow their example, I can find a happy and meaningful spiritual life one day at a time . . . and continuing through eternity.

Prayer

I pray for the strength and guidance that will enable me to live my life today as though it were my last day on this physical earth. Please grant me, dear God, the vision and wisdom to see and understand your will for me so that I may live it in my "eternal life."

Meditation

Am I really trying to live this day as though it were the last day of my earthly life?

Willingness Trumps Willpower

———————

Cowboy movies and books sometimes feature a wrangler who has to "break" a wild horse, subduing its natural spirit so that it will accept a saddle and a rider. The wrangler generally uses ropes and often gentle words and whispers to bring the wild mustang into submission.

There is a parallel here for alcoholics and addicts like myself. One of the greatest gifts I can offer to my Higher Power is my own wild, obstinate, and selfish will. Perhaps the most important sacrifice I can make is to bow my head in submission to God. In return, I will be given the direction I need to lead a sober life. I can stop trying to use my own power to subdue the insidious disease of alcoholism and drug addiction, and become willing to accept the direction of a Higher Power.

Like many other alcoholics before me, I was quite proud of my willpower. It enabled me to handle many things in my life for a while: hold a job, overcome obstacles, and persevere under difficult circumstances. I was almost certain that my strong willpower could help me control my drinking. When it failed me, I blamed my lack of control on other people and circumstances.

I fought alcohol and drugs to the bitter end, still believing that somehow my willpower would rescue me. But it didn't. It only prolonged my slide into the black pit of addiction. It wasn't until I finally became willing to admit I had a problem and sought help that I began to find a solution. In the end, my willingness trumped my willpower.

Like the wild mustang fighting the wrangler, I had to become willing to surrender in order to find some peace, comfort, and freedom from my torment. I had to squelch my own will to end the conflict and begin a new way of living in the Twelve Step program of Alcoholics Anonymous.

As I started to work the Steps, I slowly came to understand that my goal was to get rid of self-will run riot and replace it with a God-centered willingness to do whatever it takes to grow in recovery. When I reached the Eleventh Step, I found it gave me the strength and determination to seek and to do the will of my Higher Power. Prayer and meditation breathed new life into me. I began to heal as my willingness soared into trust and my trust into faith. I found a Power that replaced my own willpower.

When I began to learn more and more about how to stay sober, I came to realize how often I thought I knew enough to get by. Then I heard in the rooms of my Twelve Step program that many alcoholics and addicts have all the answers but don't really understand the questions. I saw myself in them.

The willingness to finally admit that there is always more to learn required humility and openness on my part. I found it through my many experiences with failure and defeat. When I turn to my Higher Power in ignorance, admitting I know all too little about living a spiritual life, God inspires me and sets me on the right path.

Willingness can open the door to self-discipline, something that was severely lacking in my drinking life and difficult to acquire in my new sober life. But without self-discipline, I can easily fall back into my old behaviors and my old way of thinking. Without the willingness to discipline myself, I may slack off on working the Twelve Steps in my life, reading AA's Big Book or the NA textbook, making meetings, and getting on my knees every morning to practice the Eleventh Step. Even prayer and meditation might become a chore, and soon I'll be back to doing without the very things that brought me peace and sobriety in the first place.

I have no idea at this moment just how great my life can be if I remain willing to do what it takes to maintain my sobriety. In my quiet time of communion with my Higher Power, I am given the inspiration and intuition to take the creative actions necessary to face, endure, and successfully overcome the trials of daily living and rise above them. My self-esteem is then restored because God is leading me on a spiritual journey.

God's love is the answer to all my problems. I should pray for the willingness to reach out and ask my Higher Power each day, "What is it you want me to do?" The answer will be that God wants me to willingly concentrate on helping others rather than myself by carrying AA's message of spiritual recovery from alcoholism and drug addiction.

Prayer

Please, dear God, give me the inspiration, desire, and strength to seek and follow your ways so that I no longer have to rely on my own willpower. Give me the opportunity to help others just as you have helped me.

Meditation

What am I doing each day to build my self-discipline?

Facing Life on Life's Terms

Everyone arrives at a point sometime in life when reality seems too big to cope with, when problems have gotten totally out of control, when it seems there is no way anything will ever work out. My drinking and drugging magnified that seeming reality to the point of utter hopelessness and despair.

The actuality of my life and surroundings was blurred considerably by my addiction. The truth is, the world is not nearly as vast and threatening as I may have perceived it to be. When I live just for today, my world is my house or apartment, my office or shop, my town or city. And it consists of a relatively small number of people—my family, relatives, friends, fellow Twelve Step program members, and co-workers.

The menacing nightmare I once experienced when thinking my problems were insurmountable and would go on forever was the result of regretting the past and fearing the future. I was never living in the now—for today. The program of Alcoholics Anonymous helps me to understand that I can only take one breath at a time, think one thought at a time, do one thing at a time. That's why the answer to facing life on life's terms is simply to do it one day at a time.

It wasn't until I came into my Twelve Step program and accepted this simple yet vital concept that I was finally able to face my troubles without cringing in fear. I discovered I could cope with something for one day that I couldn't do for a week, a month, or a year. And then through the Twelve Steps of recovery, I found a Higher Power I could call upon for the strength I needed to confront the reality of my life and not run away from it any longer.

Through prayer and meditation I come to understand that the true problems I have are within me—my character defects and shortcomings—and that the solution lies in the actions I take, not in the thinking I do. The constant practice of the Eleventh Step gives me the courage to face life on life's terms by first facing myself and asking God to remove my defects and shortcomings. By seeking and obeying God's will, I replace my fears with faith and continue to move ahead on my spiritual path.

It has taken me a long time to recognize the fact that most of my problems are of my own making. All the while that I was blaming other people, bad luck, and God's disapproval of my actions, the difficulties I had grew beyond my ability to solve them myself. I was lost and didn't know which way to turn.

I now look at a problem as a set of circumstances that threaten my well-being. Circumstances usually consist of people and things. Therefore, solving a problem means working with people and things in such a way as to remove the trouble from my life. Sometimes I can do it, but often I can't. That's why I need to rely on my Higher Power, who can do for me what I can't do for myself. The daily practice of the Eleventh Step will build a trusting relationship with God so that I can feel comfortable asking for help and following my Creator's will for me.

To face life on life's terms, I should ask my Higher Power each day to give me the ability to take people and things as they are. I can change myself, but rarely can I change others. I should also ask God to lead me to a frame of mind in which I would not want things to be otherwise, even if I could. Only God is powerful enough to control all things, and I will only create more problems if I try to control them myself.

As I kneel each day in prayer and meditation, I should make it a practice to discuss with my Higher Power whatever is bothering me. When thinking about a particular problem, I should ask myself if there's anything I can do about it right now, today. If there is, I should do it right away. If there's nothing I can do about it, I should simply accept it and turn it over to God. That is truly facing life on life's terms.

Prayer

Dear God, please remove from me all the fears I may have in facing another new day. Show me what I must do to become and remain physically, mentally, emotionally, and spiritually strong to meet life's challenges. Give me the grace to grow in my recovery from alcohol and other drugs, and to enjoy each new sober day you give me.

Meditation

What actions am I taking today to resolve any problems I may have in my life?

WEEK 35

An Enthusiastic Approach

There was a study done some years ago showing that, no matter what your IQ is, your attitude can make a difference when
it comes to succeeding in life. The study suggested that a person with an IQ of only 95 to 100 but having a positive, optimistic, and cooperative attitude can win more respect, earn
more money, and achieve greater success than can his or her
negative, pessimistic, uncooperative counterpart with an IQ
of 120 or more. It showed clearly that enthusiasm makes a
tremendous difference in whatever life situation I may face.

Enthusiasm releases ambition that helps carry me over hurdles
I might otherwise never leap. It endows the ups and downs of
my daily life with comeback strength and keeps me going
when the going gets tough. That's the feeling my Higher
Power gives me each day when I kneel in prayer and meditation, practicing the Eleventh Step. God raises my spirits and
gives me the enthusiasm to carry the message of recovery to
others as well as to live it myself. I am inspired to cooperate
with God's love in order to strengthen and build my spiritual
life.

As I begin to grow in sobriety, hope returns, and with it a feeling deep inside that everything will be okay as long as I work
the Steps of the AA program. Soon these hopeful feelings
turn into a positive attitude. I am filled with gratitude for my
Higher Power's generosity—giving me a life beyond my
wildest dreams. Soon this whole new attitude flows over into

119

laughter, cheer, and great enthusiasm for living the Twelve Step program.

This growing enthusiasm has the capacity for generating tremendous excitement for life, love for the people around me, eagerness to carry the message of recovery, and a desire to do God's will in all things. The reason my enthusiasm is so important is that, as a sober person, I respond to the stimuli of life not only with my five senses and my brain but also with my emotions. I am alive in proportion to how much I care; when I stop caring, part of me seems to die.

Since the fountain of my enthusiasm today is my relationship with my Higher Power, rather than with alcohol and drugs, it is more than simply excitement. It involves deep affection for what aroused it—God and the program of Alcoholics Anonymous. And when I feel that kind of enthusiasm, I return it with love.

Being good to people and being enthusiastic go hand in hand. Enthusiasm is a magic spark that transforms just "being" into "living." It makes hard work easy. There is no better tonic for depression, no greater elixir than enthusiasm for whatever happens to be wrong at the moment.

When I have this kind of positive attitude, I find it easier to have harmonious relationships with family, friends, and co-workers, as well as with all those in my Twelve Step fellowship. I see that most of the time my feelings no longer depend upon what happens outside of me but rather what happens inside. I meet the problems of life with a different spirit. My moods are not dependent on having a full wallet or pocketbook or the approval of others, but rather on the quality of my relationship with God and my fellow humans.

Enthusiasm and spirituality are very much aligned. People who are close to God are usually happy people. As an observer of Mother Teresa once said, "I never saw Mother without a smile. She could be serving the sick and the poor under the most squalid conditions, yet her smile would turn her surroundings into the Garden of Eden or the gates of Heaven."

True spirituality is an enthusiastic way of life. I don't just think about it or feel it or sense it around me, I live it. This spirituality permeates the very core of my being, affecting the way I perceive the world, the way I see my life, and the choices I make based on my perceptions and sensations.

The more I seek to grow spiritually, the more enthusiastic I will be about life and about passing that enthusiasm on to other people. I will continue to do as the AA program suggests: turn my will and my life over to the care of my Higher Power so that I can be guided into taking the right actions. It is those actions that lead me into thinking right, and it is through thinking right that I am filled with gratitude, enthusiasm, and love for God and the people in my life.

Prayer

Dear God, I know you are the true source of the enthusiasm growing within me for the Twelve Step program and the spiritual life it has given me. I ask for the grace to maintain and improve my positive attitude so that I can be even more willing to serve you in any way I can.

Meditation

Am I truly enthusiastic about my sobriety and the Twelve Step way of life, or is there something holding me back?

Progress, Not Perfection

————⟨✦⟩————

Once I accept the fact that I am not now nor ever will be perfect, I am well on my way to making progress in my recovery from my addiction to alcohol and other drugs. For it was my unrealistic need to be perfect that stood in the way of my sobriety. Perfectionism imposes impossible tasks and goals that guarantee failure.

When I finally came into the Twelve Step program of Alcoholics Anonymous, I was told that mistakes can be regarded as learning experiences, not dire signs never to try again. I discovered that accepting my own limitations made me more tolerant of the faults of those around me. And when I found a Higher Power through AA's Twelve Steps of recovery, I was happy to learn that God accepts and loves me as I am.

The Eleventh Step enhances my progress in sobriety, since it guides me and focuses me on the essential path to recovery—a spiritual life. Through the daily practice of prayer and meditation, my Higher Power gives me the strength and courage to face all the obstacles I must overcome in order to make spiritual progress.

I have also come to understand that my Twelve Step program is not a cocoon, a place to hide from the world. It is a place where I learn how to stay clean and sober so that I can live comfortably and make progress in the world outside the fellowship. In recovery, I lose the tendency to seek only safe places and easy tasks. Instead, I develop the courage with God's help to wrestle with the toughest problems and difficulties. I gain the flexibility to adjust and adapt myself to the changing patterns of life.

As a strong, sober person, I can break the chain of routine and renew my life by reading new books, traveling to new places, making new friends, taking up new hobbies, and adopting new viewpoints. I come to recognize that the only ceiling life has is the one I give it, that I am surrounded by infinite possibilities for growth and achievement. I know that if it is the will of God for me, I can accomplish great things and fulfill my most cherished dreams.

But progress doesn't always mean being busy doing things: working on another new project, setting up and cleaning up at meetings, making coffee and running errands, or being constantly on the phone or computer. Quiet times of solitude are just as important, or perhaps even more so.

How often, for example, have I come to the end of a day—or a week or month—only to discover that I've spent little or no time alone with my Higher Power? Television, the Internet, meetings, chores, and a cacophony of other "noises" have crowded out prayer and meditation.

When this occurs, I must try to recognize that I am slipping backward in the most important area of my sobriety: my spiritual life. Immediately I should redouble my efforts in the practice of the Eleventh Step and get into the habit of using prayer and meditation on a daily basis to improve my relationship with God.

As I continue to stay clean and sober, I see clearly that my Higher Power has given me two important gifts to help me progress in my recovery: a guiding spirit and the power of choice to go forward or to return to the drunken abyss from which I came. When I choose to move forward, God's power is available to help me. It is up to me to use it.

The need I once had to be perfect does not always go completely away. That's why I can get so down on myself when I foul up, make another mistake, or do something that I know contradicts the will of my Higher Power. To grow in sobriety, I must continually strive to take the right actions no matter how many times I might fail. I must keep recognizing that God loves me no matter what and will always help me whenever I ask.

One important way of measuring my progress is to remember my past, the power my addiction had over me, and then how my recovery began.

If I remember how I acted then, I will see the difference in my behavior today. I don't think or act like an alcoholic or drug addict any longer. I was lonely then; today I am surrounded by real friends. My relationships were broken; today they are healed or being healed. I was filled with self-pity; today my happiness and joy are growing as I put more effort into practicing the Eleventh Step. My past was filled with anger and resentment; today I am filled with love and gratitude. Yes, I have made progress, but I must continue on because the battle against my addiction to alcohol and drugs—an incurable disease—is never completely won.

Prayer

Please help me to find true humility so that I can eliminate completely any need to be perfect. Help me, dear God, to continue making progress in my spiritual life so that I can remain sober and useful to you in helping others.

Meditation

Am I pleased with the progress I am making in working my Twelve Step program, or am I overly critical of my efforts to the point of undermining my sobriety?

God, My Best Friend

———◦◦◦———

A true friend is someone who cares for me through thick and thin, always gives me the benefit of the doubt, and never deserts me in good times or in bad. Such a person is a rare gift indeed.

It's important to recognize, however, that even the best friend in the entire world is not perfect and can still let me down at times, often because I let him or her down. There is only one true friend I can never let down, one absolutely true friend who will never let me down. That one is God.

Every experience from my past, the fact that I survived the disease of alcoholism and other drug addiction and am now on the road to recovery, tells me loudly and clearly that my Higher Power wants to be my best friend. Still, the notion that God would want me as a best friend may be difficult to understand at first until I look closely at what that relationship is based on. It is based on the love of my Creator. Since most human parents love their children deeply, how much more must my Higher Power love me? Infinitely more, and it's a love I can continue to experience.

Each day as I practice the Eleventh Step of AA in my life, I have the opportunity to express my love for my Higher Power in return by asking to know God's will and the power to carry it out. Prayer and meditation are expressions of my love and friendship for my Creator, as well as of gratitude for having such a great friend.

There is no way I can ever pay God back for this indescribable sober life I've been given, not to mention the promise that the best is yet to come if I stay the course. At least that's true from my human perspective. But it's not true from a spiritual point of view.

While there's no way I can match God's loving friendship and great generosity, I can strive to live each day expressing that friendship and love toward others. I can share the blessings of my recovery by carrying the Twelve Step message to other suffering alcoholics and addicts. I can try to be as good a friend to them as God is to me.

When it comes to human relationships, I often know much about my friends. However, when it comes to my Higher Power, even though I've experienced God's saving grace and continuing loving support, how often have I asked, "Who is God? What is God really like? How can I come to know more about God?"

I see the beauty of flowering trees, the majesty of the star-filled sky, the magnificence of the mountains, and the glory of the seas. I wonder who fixed the progression of the day and night and who ordered the procession of the seasons. Each day I face the miracle of life and the mystery of death. In the midst of these and so many more wonders, all my limited human mind can comprehend is that it's the work of an awesome Creator the world has been praising since time began.

But while my mind cannot fully see, feel, or comprehend such a spiritual deity, I know from my own human experience that this Higher Power has touched my life in a deeply personal way. I know, therefore, that God is not some undefined, far-off universal force, but rather is right here with me, within me, around me—offering me the kind of spiritual love that can protect me, guide me, and bring me into a life of the spirit.

The best way for me to come to know God in a personal way is through daily prayer and meditation. Practice of the Eleventh Step can help make me intimately aware of God's presence in my heart, where I can share everything that is in me and receive in return everything I need. But my prayer must contain an attitude of humility, a willing acceptance that my whole life and everything in it depends on my Higher Power.

As my best friend, God has promised to provide for all my needs. All I have to do is petition in heartfelt prayer and ask that my joy may be full. I must remember, however, that my Higher Power knows better than I what I need. So no matter what I pray for, God will never give me anything that could harm me or lead me astray. That is truly a best friend.

Prayer

Dear God, I truly believe you are my best friend. That is why I want to know you more. Please bless me with the desire and determination to make the Eleventh Step of AA an important part of my daily life so that I can draw closer to you and come to know your will for me in all things.

Meditation

What do I do each day to express my gratitude for God's great friendship?

The Myth of Self-Reliance

Perhaps the most difficult thing I've had to do in my life thus far in order to get well was to admit and accept the fact that I am powerless over alcohol and drugs. But for someone whose very existence once centered on self-reliance, admitting I was powerless was like losing my equilibrium or winding up with a severe case of vertigo.

I had always believed, despite my losing battle with my addiction, that I was still in charge—that somehow I could still control my own life and the people and situations around me, that if I couldn't depend on myself, than I could depend on no one.

Then I found God through the program of Alcoholics Anonymous and everything changed. By coming into my Twelve Step program and turning my will and my life over to the care of a Higher Power, self-reliance now seems like a myth. I have found that by subjugating my will to the will of God, I have the power I once sought in other things—booze, drugs, money, sex. And I am being directed along a spiritual path where I find the kind of balance and confidence in life I never had before.

In place of self-reliance I have found self-discipline. It enables me to move through each day with a sure sense that I will get where I am going. It removes the doubts I once had. It gives me the strength to take the right actions that keep me away from alcohol and other drugs, and keeps me close to my Higher Power.

I get all this by practicing the Eleventh Step on a daily basis. In my prayers and meditation, I ask for the grace to rely on God's direction and inspiration instead of on my own thinking and inclinations. I ask God to help me be more self-disciplined in making the right choices and doing the things required of me to stay sober.

It takes discipline to say no when I need to, when perhaps every fiber in my being may be urging me to give in again. It takes discipline to stand up and be counted in the face of difficult challenges when my pattern was to shirk my responsibilities.

When I rid myself of my past obstinate self-reliance by practicing the Eleventh Step, God appears within me and restores my trust. That trust in my Higher Power can provide me with the weapons to restrain my ego and free me from the bondage of self.

When I finally stop trying to run my own life and give God a chance, I come to understand that I am not being offered some elaborate, complicated plan for living, one with many twists and turns and filled with unrealistic demands. God's plan for me is simple—to be a sober and loving person. That plan may call me to a certain job or relationship where I am more challenged. But my Higher Power's will for me is still very simple—to be an obedient and loving servant.

When I surrender myself, God will make sure that my life is in line with a spiritual plan beyond my understanding, a plan filled with blessings that will bring great satisfaction to all that I do.

As I grow spiritually by relying on God's will, I find that my former attitudes toward self-centered goals have to undergo drastic revisions. My demands for emotional security and material gains, for personal prestige and power, have to be redefined and redirected into more generous and loving pursuits.

Through AA's Eleventh Step, I learn that the satisfaction of those selfish pursuits cannot be the singular end and main purpose of my life. When I am willing to place spiritual growth first, then I have a real chance of learning how to love—and then how to share that love with other people and with God.

As I continue to grow in my spiritual program through the practice of AA's Twelve Steps, I change from being self-reliant to being God-reliant. All I need to do is remember that God has all the power and that power is there to help me live a sober, healthy, and loving life.

Prayer

My overemphasis on self-reliance blinded me from a new way of living until my addiction totally defeated me. Dear God, please help me to learn from this experience that you have the answers to the kind of life I both want and need. Give me the grace to live according to your will for me every day.

Meditation

Am I willing today to let go and let God, or does my ingrained self-reliance still cause me problems?

Trusting My Conscience

———⟐———

Many people regard their conscience as an innate repository of values and opinions about what is right or wrong, an internal sense that is subjective and personal, and which no one else can correct. Since I am imperfect, however, my conscience can also be imperfect. Therefore, how can I trust it to guide me correctly in all my judgments, choices, and decisions?

The answer for me today is simple. By practicing the Twelve Steps of Alcoholics Anonymous, I develop what is called "an informed conscience." This means that after taking a searching and fearless moral inventory and after admitting and discussing my character defects and shortcomings with another person, I will have a much clearer sense of what is right and what is wrong. The self-will and self-deception that once fogged my thinking as an active alcoholic or drug addict will gradually dissipate and be removed from my life.

Prayer and meditation on the Eleventh Step will help me build a close and trusting relationship with my Higher Power. That trust will inspire me to follow the right actions modeled by more experienced members of my Twelve Step program. Those actions will not only lead me into right thinking, but they will also help shape my conscience, thus preventing me from making erroneous, self-serving judgments about what I should do or say, or how I should live my life today and tomorrow.

All this may sound quite simple, but it's not always easy. I can still be dominated by self-interest because, like most alcoholics and drug addicts, I have a tendency to be selfish and self-centered. That's why in my daily practice of the Eleventh Step, I must ask for the strength to do what is pleasing to God and my fellow man ahead of what is pleasing to me. If I can truly say I am seeking to do God's will instead of mine, then I can trust my conscience because it will be directed by my Higher Power.

Even though I can now—with God's help—trust my conscience in difficult decisions, it's always a good idea to seek the advice of others I trust, such as my sponsor, family, close friends, or a spiritual leader. Also, the more I pray with humility to my Higher Power, the more I will be able to hear God speak to me in the depths of my heart.

As I develop "an informed conscience," one I can trust, my integrity will grow. I will find it easier to treat people fairly and honestly. My old behavior of cheating or fudging the truth will make me uncomfortable, and I will want to rid it completely from my life. With integrity, I will give my word and keep it. I will be direct and up-front, and not say things simply to please people.

If I find myself surrounded by dishonesty or immorality, I will confront it whenever possible. If that doesn't work, I will move on in order to protect my own reputation and my own soul. I may not receive immediate rewards from those around me for my integrity, but God will reward me with a peaceful conscience for living right.

It's in the Eleventh Step that daily prayer and meditation provide the truth and inspiration my conscience requires to guide me. It deflects my mind from the problems I am experiencing and raises my thoughts above the grievances and discontent that color and cloud my thinking. It's in my quiet times of spiritual seeking that great truths and realizations are born. They are seldom born in the crowded, noisy auditoriums of life.

The messages I receive when practicing the Eleventh Step are specifically for my will and my conscience, not necessarily for my head. That's why the power of God begins to work in me the moment I become open and willing to have my disposition and behavior altered and changed.

Through my growing relationship with my Higher Power, I am now better able to listen and take direction. My addiction made me a negative person. Now God is helping me to change my perceptions and embrace positive thoughts so that my informed conscience can guide me along the path of my new spiritual life.

Prayer

May I become totally willing to accept your direction and inspiration, dear God, so that I can trust and rely upon my sober conscience as I try to live a spiritual life. Through your grace, please give me the integrity I need to live honestly and lovingly with you and my fellow man.

Meditation

Can I trust my conscience today to make the right choices and decisions that improve my sobriety and spiritual growth?

One Day at a Time

———⸻———

One of the greatest prayers ever taught, going back two thousand years, contains an essential request that helps me focus on living in the now: "Give us this day our daily bread."

I am not instructed to ask God to fulfill my needs for a week, a month, or a year. I am directed to ask for just what I need for today. That is why I must strive to live my entire life that way—one day at a time.

My addiction to alcohol and other drugs took away my ability to live in and enjoy each day. I became so remorseful of the past and so fearful of the future that I was constantly terrorized by what another day might bring. But when I finally started really working my Twelve Step program, I found I no longer had to live in a constant state of remorse and fear. By turning my life and my will over to a Power greater than myself, I found a whole new concept of living.

I came to understand that today is the only day I have. There is no guarantee of tomorrow, and yesterday, with all its mistakes and sorrows, is gone forever. Today, this present moment, is infinitely precious.

But even though I have come to recognize and understand how important each new day is, I can still waste it by spending time living in the past and worrying about the future unless I continually practice the Eleventh Step. Through daily prayer and meditation, God will help me live each moment to the fullest by focusing on the needs of others rather than on my own. It's only my concern about self that takes me out of the present.

When I was adrift in my addiction, I took my sordid circumstances and myself very seriously, often to the point where I lost contact with reality. Eventually, there was no joy or humor, no real satisfaction in much of what I did. Everything around me became grim and dark. Today, by trying to forget self and seek God's will, positive signs of spiritual rebirth are growing in my life.

Each new day I gain more spiritual energy and zest for life. I find joy and humor in others and myself. Laughter shows that I am getting sober and healthy, that I am alive again and on my way to real recovery through God and the Twelve Step program.

Certainly not every day will be a bed of roses. I will always have my share of pain and disappointment, but with the help of my Higher Power, I can handle it without a drink or a drug. Preoccupation with the past and the future will not let me avoid the pain of the present. The only real solution is to pause, look deeply within myself, face today's problems with rigorous honesty, and make the choices the day demands, knowing God is with me.

The burdens of my yesterdays can often be too great for me to bear alone. Also, if I think of my life in terms of all the things I must do tomorrow, next week, or next year, the sheer weight of the resulting worry could overwhelm me. Before I know it,

I could be thinking about a drink or a drug to ease the stress. Whenever I find myself approaching this frame of mind, I must stop immediately and ask my Higher Power to bring me back to the now, to bring me back to today, where the burdens are more manageable and where I can either do something about them or accept them when I can't.

Planning is certainly a normal, healthy function. It is also a necessary function to help me keep my life manageable at work, at home, and in all my affairs. But when planning leads me into projecting the outcome of my plans, I am headed for trouble. For when I project, I tend not to visualize the good things the future might hold. I am more likely to project problems and, based on my past, assume that some tragedy looms ahead.

The present moment can be large and interesting enough to occupy all my attention if I can learn to focus on it. Now that I am sober and productive again, my life is filled with enormous opportunities. Each day as I kneel in prayerful meditation on the Eleventh Step, I should ask God to show me these opportunities and give me the power and courage to undertake them, and by so doing, to improve my spiritual life and help others find what I've found—an incredible way to live each day, one day at a time.

Prayer

Dear God, please teach me to live in the now, to use each day to enjoy my sobriety while being open and willing to help others for your sake. Let me no longer regret the past or fear the future, because today I am in your loving hands.

Meditation

How successful am I at living one day at a time? What can I do to be even more successful?

Unconditional Love

⟶⟶⟶⟶⟶⟶

The most powerful force in the entire universe is unconditional love. Its awesome beneficial consequences are too overwhelming to ever be fully understood, measured, or defined. To love or be loved unconditionally is the epitome of a spiritual life.

While it may be difficult to comprehend that kind of love, the one thing we can be certain of is that God is the source of unconditional love. As the one who created me, my Higher Power loves me just as I am, without conditions. All God asks in return is that I strive to love others the very same way.

When I look back, I now realize that it was God's love that enabled me to survive my terrible ordeal with alcohol and other drugs and then led me to recovery through the Twelve Steps of Alcoholics Anonymous.

As I practice the Eleventh Step each day, I have a growing sense of the tremendous power of love, both the unconditional love of God and the unconditional love I find in the rooms of my Twelve Step fellowship. I discover that there is no difficulty that love cannot conquer, no pain that love cannot soothe, no door that love will not open, no gulf that love will not bridge, and no wall that love cannot knock down.

It makes no difference how deeply seated the trouble may be, how hopeless the outlook, how great the mistake. True unconditional love will dissolve it all, because loving this way enables me to forgive the deepest hurts, resolve the strongest resentments, and rebuild relationships that have been torn asunder. It's the healing salve for the most painful wounds.

By seeking God's help and strength through the Eleventh Step to practice unconditional love, I find myself becoming more willing to forgive injuries not just in words, but also in my heart. I don't do this simply for the sake of the other person. I do this for myself, because resentment, condemnation, anger, and the desire for someone else to be punished are feelings and thoughts that rob me of my own serenity and sobriety. Forgiveness sets me free and fills me with the self-esteem my addiction once stole from me.

Unconditional love is not necessarily sparked by positive emotional feelings. In fact, often they are lacking. Unconditional love is a decision of the will, both in intention and in action. That's why when I turn my will over to God's care in the Third Step and then continue to seek God's will in the Eleventh Step, I am given the strength to make loving decisions even in the most difficult situations.

Being given this great gift by my Higher Power makes it easier for me to admit my own faults, be more tolerant of others, and make amends even to those I don't particularly like. Since God loves everyone, I should do my best to do the same.

While God's love will never fail me, sometimes my obstinate refusal to share that love with others will set back my spiritual growth. When my prayers are not being answered, it may be because I am lacking a sense of love for others. If I watch my thoughts, my tongue, and my actions each day, I can tell how sincerely I am trying to share God's love.

There may be times when I go through a difficult period, when I find my life becoming complicated or suddenly filled with problems. I may feel some distance between God and myself. It could affect my mood. I may lash out at others for no real reason. That's when I must remember that even when darkness seems to surround me, my Higher Power's love for me never dims. If I continue to practice the Eleventh Step each day, seeking God's power through prayer and meditation, my faith will always see me through.

A teacher once asked a group of children, ages four to eight, what love meant to them. Some of their replies were quite insightful: "Love is when you eat at McDonald's and give someone most of your french fries without asking for any back." "Love is when Mommy sips Daddy's coffee to make sure it tastes good before giving it to him." "Love is what makes you smile when you're tired." "Love is what's in the parlor at Christmas when you stop opening presents and look around."

I may not be as loving as I think I am if I haven't consciously chosen to show that love. In other words, good intentions are not always an expression of unconditional love. At the same time, whenever I actually exert myself to really love someone, it reflects the will of my Higher Power and enhances my spiritual growth.

Prayer

Thank you, dear God, for saving me through your unconditional love. Please give me the willingness to share that love with others so I can grow spiritually and carry the great message of recovery to others suffering from addiction.

Meditation

What actions do I take each day to ensure that I am sharing God's unconditional love with others?

Making Amends

Was I the kind of person who would staunchly declare that my addiction never hurt anyone? That my family never suffered because I always paid the bills and seldom drank or did drugs at home? That I never really wronged anyone at work or harmed the company (even though I would take days off to recover from another bout)? So what was all the complaining about if I hadn't done any real damage to anyone?

It took a lot of pain and humiliation to finally smash this attitude of self-justification and purposeful forgetting. The rigorous honesty I found in the Twelve Step program of Alcoholics Anonymous forced me to search and examine my motives and actions, and to face the truth about myself. And the truth was that my addiction caused me to harm many over a long period of time.

It was difficult to admit at first the pain and hurt all my defects of character and shortcomings had caused others. But working the Twelve Steps of AA cleared my vision, showed me the things I needed to change, gave me the tools to do it, and set me on a spiritual path of recovery. My feelings of shame and guilt began to lift, my fear and isolation lessened, and my sense of self-respect and self-esteem gradually returned.

However, it soon became evident that I could not make much headway along the spiritual path to sobriety until I made an honest and accurate survey of the human wreckage I left in the wake of my addiction. When I began to take a searching and fearless moral inventory of myself, it became immediately clear that my claim of not really hurting anyone was an absolute lie. It was the epitome of self-deception. I found much damage to repair and many direct amends to make.

The wonderful prospect of living in peace and harmony with family, friends, and members of my Twelve Step fellowship spurred my determination to clean up the past. I found that making amends had to come from my heart, not my head. Before starting on this emotional journey, I discussed its possible pitfalls with friends in the program and received guidance from my sponsor. But most of all, I put myself into the hands of my Higher Power, asking for the strength and inspiration to handle the task.

I found that by practicing the Eleventh Step and seeking God's help through prayer and meditation, I was given the courage to persevere even when the going got difficult. I learned from the experience of my fellow travelers that those I must make amends to include my family, friends, co-workers, neighbors, creditors, and people who are deceased or otherwise unavailable—usually in that order.

While staying sober is the single greatest thing I can do to make amends to my family, that doesn't mean I can ignore the serious emotional or physical damage I've done. I must repair it in every way possible: by always being there for them, calming their fears, doing positive things with and for them, and expressing the unconditional love God has taught me through my Twelve Step program.

If my family is still intact, making amends, while difficult, can prove to be a very satisfying and fulfilling experience. However, if I've lost my family through my addiction, I must still try to the best of my ability to heal the wounds even if reconciling is not possible.

I should approach those friends and other significant people in my life with honesty and humility, admitting the pain I caused them through my addiction but not using addiction as an excuse. I simply want to express my good intentions, admit my regrets, and promise to make whatever amends are called for. If I am rebuffed, I ask my Higher Power to help me accept that response without feelings of anger or resentment. If my amends are accepted, I should thank God for all the help and guidance.

With my creditors, I should lay my cards on the table. If immediate payment is possible, I should try to arrange the best deal I can. If the sum is too large, I should work out a payment schedule I know I can meet. It's important that I'm as honest with myself as I can be about what I owe and to whom. Trying to justify myself or practice self-deception can only lead me back down the path of lies, blame, and another drink or drug.

Practice of the Eleventh Step can be an enormous help when it comes to making amends to those I've harmed who are unavailable. I must turn the self-condemnation and guilt I feel over to my Higher Power. Having remorse over amends I cannot make personally is futile. But I can make amends by offering prayers for them—if deceased, at their graveside if possible—asking my Higher Power to bless them.

Prayer

God, please grant me the desire to make amends to all I have harmed in any way through my addiction. Bless me with the self-honesty not only to repair the damage, but to share with all those I've hurt the unconditional love you have placed in my heart.

Meditation

Is there any person with whom or situation where I am hesitant to make amends? What do I plan to do about it?

Anger and Resentment

———⟫⊙⟪———

When Achilles, one of the heroes of Greek mythology, was born, his mother plunged him into the river Styx, which made his whole body invulnerable, except for the heel by which she held him. It was a wound to Achilles' heel in battle that finally killed him.

For an alcoholic or drug addict like myself, anger and resentment form the "Achilles' heel" of my disease. If I am not vigilant, those negative emotions can quickly lead me back into the battle with my addiction and kill me. They are that powerful an enemy.

Anger can multiply my difficulties in many situations. I can look back and remember the times when I exacerbated my problems by stepping on the gas, reaching the speed of rage, and losing all ability to apply the brakes. In the insanity of my disease, there were times when I felt energized by letting my anger fly, almost enjoying the power it gave me despite the damage I caused.

The Twelve Steps of recovery began teaching me how to manage my feelings, control my outbursts, and calm my anger before it turns into a resentment, which simply means feeling that anger over and over again. Today I seek another kind of power—the power of God. By working the Eleventh Step in my life on a daily basis, I ask my Higher Power through prayer and meditation to remove my Achilles' heel and replace it with faith and understanding. When I turn my life and my will over to the care of God, I begin to lose the unreasonable fear that used to fuel my anger, and I find some peace and serenity.

However, since my addiction once made me a perfectionist in the art of self-deception, I can still at times hide my anger and resentment even from myself. I must be vigilant, for vigilance can alert me to unexpressed anger that manifests itself in sarcasm, cynicism, or flippancy in conversation; overpoliteness or a grin-and-bear-it attitude; difficulty in falling asleep; excessive irritability over trifles; clenched jaws; or a chronic stiff or sore neck.

All these negative experiences are undesirable at best and destructive at worst. They are certainly signs that something has gone awry with my spiritual life. Perhaps I have stopped praying in the Eleventh Step for knowledge of God's will and the power to carry it out. Perhaps I have slowed my progress in seeking a closer relationship with my Higher Power, who is the source of my peace and serenity, who can eliminate my fears.

The Eleventh Step keeps me aware of those character defects and shortcomings that can spark my anger. It clears my vision so that I can be honest and see the truth about myself, the truth that can free me from my negative feelings and impulses.

It's the anger and resentment I'm prone to that can do the most damage to my sobriety and to the relationships I'm trying to set right. The presence of any signs that these feelings have crept back into my life should be enough to get me to take a good look at myself and, through the Eleventh Step, ask God's help to be rigorously honest.

I should also stay close to my sponsor and good friends in the fellowship, for they can usually spot changes in my behavior before I'm aware of them myself. This is often how my Higher Power guides me back onto a spiritual path, the only path that can lead me away from anger and resentment, and toward healing of those negative emotions.

Prayer

I pray that you, my God, may always keep me aware of any unexpressed anger and resentment. I know today that my "Achilles' heel" is a deadly force that can lead me away from you and thwart my spiritual progress. Help me to stay close to you and the Twelve Step program, where I can continue to enjoy my sobriety and my peace of mind.

Meditation

How often do I search inside myself for any signs of anger and resentment, and if I find them, what actions do I take?

Carrying the Message

———⟫●⟪———

There is no greater satisfaction, no deeper joy, no stronger sense of gratitude than that which comes from carrying my Twelve Step program's message of sobriety to another suffering alcoholic or addict. And then to watch that person awaken to the presence of a Higher Power, to see hope and faith light his or her visage, and to follow with wonder the miracle of recovery as it unfolds in that person's life—that is a gift God gives to anyone who seeks it wholeheartedly.

The message of the Twelve Steps is simple, yet often difficult for many to accept at first. It's simply this: there is a solution to the disease of addiction for all those ready to admit defeat and turn their wills and lives over to the care of a Power greater than themselves.

The privilege of carrying this message of recovery from alcohol and drug addiction to those seeking help is a loving gift from God and the premise upon which AA was originally founded: one alcoholic helping another. This special gift to help other suffering alcoholics isn't dependent on people's education or position in life. It was given to me and other sober alcoholics—whether physicians, factory workers, ministers, or waitresses—to teach us to live spiritually and humbly, recognizing that it's God's power, not mine, that keeps me sober.

Daily practice of the Eleventh Step prepares me to carry the message of recovery. My Higher Power gives me, through my prayers and meditation, the inspiration and the words I need when sharing my experience with those whose addiction has made them suspicious of "do-gooders," fearful of stopping drinking and drugging, and still deep in denial.

As I continue to carry the message, God often blesses me with another wonderful gift, the gift of sponsorship. I'm afforded the opportunity to share my experience, strength, and hope on an intimate basis with another human being. And while I have this great privilege of guiding another alcoholic through the Twelve Steps of recovery, I am given the added benefits of strengthening my own sobriety, keeping my memory fresh, and getting rid of any complacency that can often occur when taking sobriety for granted.

While sponsorship is a very great privilege, there are also many other ways of carrying the recovery message:

- Being a strong example of contented sobriety, both inside and outside of my Twelve Step fellowship

- Making hospital calls on members and patients

- Attending my home group meetings on a regular basis and visiting outside meetings when traveling to other towns or cities

- Making phone calls to new members

- Coming to meetings early and staying late to talk with those having problems trying to live the program

- Encouraging others to study *Alcoholics Anonymous* (the Big Book) or the NA textbook, as well as *Twelve Steps and Twelve Traditions*

- Speaking at other groups and chairing meetings at my home group

- Attending business meetings in order to help with the needs of my group

- Offering to drive people to and from meetings and to other places that can benefit their sobriety

- Telling the Twelve Step recovery story to clergy members, doctors, judges, educators, and employers, and offering to help whenever appropriate

- Talking with families, relatives, friends, and associates of active alcoholics and offering assistance where appropriate

When I look around, I often see that some of the happiest people I know are those who devote themselves to seemingly hopeless causes. I can find that happiness, too. However, in carrying the Twelve Step message of hope and recovery, I find there is really no such thing as a hopeless cause or a hopeless case. It often may seem so from many points of view, but I know that with God, nothing is hopeless or impossible.

That's why practicing the Eleventh Step in my life on a daily basis is so important. It keeps me ever mindful of God's loving power and aware that God can always do for others what has been done for me.

Prayer

Thank you, dear God, for the special privilege of carrying the message of recovery from addiction to others. I recognize what a truly magnificent gift you have given me and how it continues to sustain my sobriety. In gratitude, may I always be available to you whenever you call upon me to help another.

Meditation

The best way to keep my memory fresh and my sobriety strong is to constantly seek ways to carry the message of recovery to others. How am I doing that?

What Can I Pray For?

⸻⸳⸻

Prayer is the lifting of my mind and heart to God so that I can develop a better understanding of and closer relationship to my Higher Power. This sincere and loving communication makes me feel more comfortable when asking and thanking God for meeting and fulfilling all my needs.

When practicing the Eleventh Step, I am directed to ask my Higher Power only for knowledge of his will for me and the power to carry that out. This seeming limitation on what I can pray for results from the kinds of selfish and foolish demands that alcoholics and addicts like myself have made of God in the past, and sometimes even in the present.

When I was captive to my addiction, I was constantly asking God to bring my spouse back, help me pay the rent, get me out of another hassle, let me keep my job, make me feel better. Even when God answered my prayers, I would soon be drinking or drugging again and begging for help once more, until I finally stopped asking.

Although I'm sober today, sometimes my immediate temptation is still to pray for specific solutions to specific problems or for the ability to help other people the way I think they should be helped. While the Twelve Step program of Alcoholics Anonymous tells me that's asking God to do it "my way," I still have the tendency to think I know what's best for me and for others in my life. However, no matter how well-intentioned these requests are, they really are self-seeking rather than seeking God's will in all things.

Therefore, when asking God to consider a particular need for myself or another—whether it concerns illness, family problems, legal matters, or other serious misfortunes—let me add to each request "if it be thy will." In this way, I will be surrendering control to God and simply asking for guidance and power to help where I can, leaving the rest completely in the hands of my Higher Power.

The process of prayer and the continuing use of the Eleventh Step helps me eliminate the danger of forgetting what God does and what God expects me to do. I am responsible for taking the initiative, but I must always ask for strength and guidance from my Higher Power.

Prayer, as discussed in the Third and Eleventh Steps of AA, will enable me sooner or later to find a way out of any difficulty. My fears and insecurities disappear and are replaced by a true appreciation for sobriety and a new attitude of gratitude. And when I pray, I can use my own words or a traditional prayer.

The Lord's Prayer is from the Christian Bible, but it is often used in Twelve Step meetings. It contains a compact formula for the development of one's spiritual life. It seems to have been designed for that specific purpose, and when used regularly and with understanding, it has helped many people experience dramatic changes in their lives.

This prayer, also called the Our Father, makes it clear that my Higher Power wants me to lead a healthy, happy spiritual life, one filled with joyous and meaningful experiences. To this end, God knows I will require such things as food, clothing, and shelter; an education through books, school, and travel; and opportunities for work and relaxation. All these things God offers me under the heading of "our daily bread." But to obtain them, I have to claim them. I have to recognize that God alone is the source and all I have to do is ask. If it's the will of my Higher Power, I will receive them.

Prayer is an exercise I should undertake not only in the morning and at night. I can pause during the day when situations must be met and decisions made and renew that simple prayerful request: "Thy will, not mine, be done."

I should also have in my spiritual arsenal some favorite prayers I can turn to when experiencing an emotional disturbance or confronting a sudden and unexpected problem. Whispering a prayer over and over will often enable me to clear the channel choked up with anger, fear, frustration, or misunderstanding. It will let me return to the surest help of all—the will of my Higher Power.

By practicing the Eleventh Step in my life each day, I will intuitively begin to realize that while my spiritual path won't always be easy to tread, I can make it. The most important thing is to maintain a strong, prayerful relationship with a loving God.

Prayer

Dear God, please keep me ever mindful of the power of prayer for bringing your light, love, and spirit into my life. Help me to understand that you are the source of all good things and that my real peace and happiness come from doing your will.

Meditation

Do I still have a tendency to think that I don't need to seek God's will in my life and that I can handle everything on my own? What am I doing to change that?

God's Great Gifts

Grace is the most precious gift my Higher Power can offer me. It's like serendipity: I am unexplainably given wonderful and valuable things not sought after or earned. But God does not force grace upon me. I have my own free will. It is something I can either accept or reject.

Through all the years of my terrible addiction to alcohol and other drugs, my Higher Power was always there awaiting my willingness to listen, to reach the point where I was ready to do anything to change the way of my existence. When that day came, God was there to offer me the grace of recovery. This time I accepted. It led me into the Twelve Step program and a whole new way of living.

Yet in the beginning, despite God's grace, I thought only of my addiction lifestyle losses. Facing abstinence, I mourned the false freedom from fear and pain that alcohol and drugs gave me, the so-called drinking buddies I had to leave behind, the "bright lights" I once thought I couldn't live without. But then, as I began to build a relationship with a Higher Power through AA's Twelve Steps of recovery, I began to experience the real gifts that God provides in sobriety.

At first these gifts were simple, but still very meaningful, like a good night's sleep, improvement in my health, and a good appetite and peace of mind. For every so-called buddy I left behind, I found two real friends in the rooms of my Twelve

Step fellowship. For the bright lights I once enjoyed, I found real camaraderie in my recovery group and participation in meaningful and fun activities. For every loss I thought I had experienced, I gained a dozen blessings.

When I reached the Ninth Step, God poured out even more gifts through the promises of the Big Book of AA.[4]

I began to enjoy a new freedom and a new happiness. I no longer regretted the past or shut the door on it. I comprehended and now enjoyed serenity and peace. By sharing my own experience, I began to help others. I no longer felt useless or sorry for myself. Helping others replaced my self-seeking. As a result, I no longer feared people or economic insecurity. I now knew how to handle situations that used to baffle me. I became aware that God was doing for me what I could not do for myself.

In gratitude for all these great gifts, I started to practice the Eleventh Step on a daily basis with even more fervor. I sensed God's love welling up within me. Through prayer and meditation, my Higher Power inspired and directed me to share that love with others, both inside and outside of the fellowship. I began bringing God's love home to my family, to work, into all my activities. It lit the spiritual path I was now on and gave me the impetus and confidence to do God's will in all of my affairs.

The old adage "It's better to give than to receive" is certainly true in most respects when applied to my relationship with most people. However, in my relationship with my Higher Power, I find it better to receive than to give. Certainly I give God all my love and obedience, but if I hadn't received the gift of sobriety from my Higher Power in the first place and the spiritual strength required to sustain it, then I would have nothing to give anyone in return.

I cannot thank God enough for the gift of sobriety, for not only has it changed my entire life, but it has also affected all those around me for the better. I am now responsible to continue to share both my sobriety and all of my God-given talents for the benefit of others. That's why I ask each day through the Eleventh Step for greater knowledge of God's will for me and the power to carry it out. My Higher Power will guide me on that journey, a journey that will lead me to greater spiritual growth and personal fulfillment.

As I pray and meditate each day, I learn through the Eleventh Step that I can only keep and enjoy God's great gifts if I strive to give them away, to pass them on. As an expression of my gratitude, I must try to help others find what I was so freely given: sobriety and a new way of life.

Prayer

Dear God, may I always recognize that you are the source of all my great gifts. May my relationship with you always be colored by a deep sense of gratitude. Without your loving grace, I would have nothing to enjoy and nothing to share with others.

Meditation

**How often do I think about all the gifts
God has given me, and what do I do
to show my deep appreciation?**

When Dark Times Come

⟞⟞⟞⟞⟞

The strongest armor I have against a potential relapse is constant vigilance. That holds true for every alcoholic and drug addict in recovery. My only guarantee of sobriety is to not take a drink or drug today, to live by AA's Twelve Steps of recovery, and to practice the principles of the program in all my affairs.

I must avoid complacency and taking my sobriety for granted at all costs. Even Bill Wilson, the cofounder of Alcoholics Anonymous, who had a profound spiritual experience, almost relapsed on two separate occasions after such an experience. He went on to warn that every alcoholic must always remain on guard no matter how long he or she has been sober.

The reason is simple. I have a disease that wants to kill me, and it never sleeps. It pretends to be my friend, offering me solace when those bad times, those dark times, come. And they do come because life is filled with challenges, and as I've often heard, everyone gets a turn in the barrel.

If I think it's possible to avoid failure and misfortune because I'm now living a sober life, I've just bought a ticket to fairyland. I must understand that clearly and know what to do when my great hopes and dreams don't come to pass and I experience failure instead.

However, if I'm practicing the Eleventh Step on a daily basis, seeking through prayer and meditation God's power in my life, then I have a better chance of withstanding disappointments, even disillusionment. But if I start slacking on my daily routine and rest on my laurels, I may find myself ill-prepared when difficulties strike.

There may be times when I think I am making a real effort to have peace in my life, yet I am clearly not at peace. My Higher Power has said all I need to do is ask sincerely for help. I ask, but the bleakness is still there. I'm told all I need is a little willingness, yet I may ask myself, Haven't I done my part over and over again? Where is the help I expect from my Higher Power?

I remain still and the stress continues. I try to listen and I hear nothing. I pray and I get no response. So my faith lessens. My hopelessness rises. I begin to think I am not only a failure in life, but also a failure at working my program, the only thing so far that has kept me from giving in to my frustration, my anger, and my addiction.

I must try to understand as best I can during these dark times that hope and trust grow and increase mostly through trial, suffering, and sorrow. For this reason, darkness can often be an essential part of my spiritual journey. Trials and tribulations may actually be direct gifts from God, or they may arise out of ordinary happenings in life: sickness, business failure, job loss, separation from a loved one, other disappointments, or natural calamities. The worst trials may result from the negligence, selfishness, or wickedness of others—the same kinds of pain and suffering my addiction caused for many.

Continued trust in my Higher Power is the only way to gradually bring light into this darkness. I must also force myself to take the actions necessary to change my attitude from negative to positive. And most of all, I must continue to strengthen my armor against relapse by keeping the Eleventh Step alive in my life. Through constant prayer and meditation, God will let me know that things will change for the better if I am patient and have faith in the love of my Higher Power.

I must strive to become the kind of person who knows deep within that as long as I keep faith in God and in my Twelve Step program—no matter how frightening and discouraging those dark times may be—nothing can defeat me and lead me back to a drink or a drug.

God may well have a purpose behind every problem, using circumstances to develop my character and my spiritual life. It makes sense that my Higher Power would use circumstances, since I face them twenty-four hours a day. If I am living my life one day at a time, staying sober by using the tools of my program one day at a time, then I can face any circumstances—good or bad—and grow from them spiritually one day at a time.

All I need to remember is that whenever dark times enter my life, the act of placing complete trust in my Higher Power must be taken over and over again. "Thy will be done" expresses the single greatest step I can take to withstand the darkness, knowing that God and my program will soon rescue me. Everything passes, even the darkness.

Prayer

In those times when darkness seems to surround me and my hope begins to fade, please, dear God, let me know you are there. Help me to strengthen my faith and trust in you so that I can remain constantly vigilant against any threats my addiction may bring.

Meditation

Am I sure I'm doing everything I can to maintain my vigilance against any threats to my sobriety? Or can I do more?

The Poor Me's

I can call it the blues, having a bad day, feeling down, or any other appellation I'd like, but the truth is I'm often simply indulging in a bout of self-pity. I just don't want to admit it, either to myself or anyone else, because "the poor me's" are covering up what I don't want to face.

When I feel sorry for myself, I'm trying to avoid reality and the truth of what's going on in my life—feelings of guilt, anger, jealousy, false pride, or fear. It's often the emotion that comes when I fail to take seriously that part of the Serenity Prayer that reads "the courage to change the things I can."

Here again, when I get "the poor me's" I have probably slackened on my daily practice of the Eleventh Step. If I make the effort to increase my prayer and meditation, my Higher Power will surely lift my spirits and direct me to make the necessary changes in my thinking and in my actions to get back on a positive spiritual path.

When I fail to reach out to my Higher Power for help, it's often because I think my difficulties are the result of circumstances beyond my control. I can see no possible way in which my life can be changed for the better. What a wonderful excuse to feel sorry for myself.

But self-pity has many roots. Another is my need to be loved, sometimes like a little child who wants to be the center of the universe. So when I feel unimportant, unattractive, not noticed, and, above all, down on myself for not "measuring up" to whatever the circumstances may be, the "poor me's" take over.

That's when I have to do everything I can to turn to God for strength and understanding. I come to understand again that I am my Creator's child, one so important that I've been given the gift of a whole new life, a sober life, a spiritual life far beyond my wildest dreams. And I find God's love, that divine caring, by practicing the Eleventh Step each day. As I seek to draw closer to my Higher Power, my spirits are lifted and my self-esteem is restored.

I should not think that I'm the only one who has the impulse at times to get upset when things don't go my way, when I don't feel appreciated or get the attention I think I deserve. It can be a natural reaction to a personal misunderstanding, but it's a reaction I can't afford. When I harbor these feelings over a period of time, I become capable of taking some minor slight or some uncomplimentary words and developing them into a monumental grievance toward life in general.

But then there are real and serious problems that may come along, problems that can seem to be overwhelming, that feel hopeless to resolve. When one disaster is piled upon another, it's easy for me to believe the cards are stacked against me no matter how often I shuffle the deck. That feeling of hopelessness can easily give way to "the poor me's," and before I realize it, I'm in a state where I find it very difficult to take any decisive action. It launches a terrible cycle of frustration, aggression, fear, and more self-pity.

There is another avenue of the "poor me's" I must also try to avoid: when I become so afraid of failure that I turn the difficulties of a situation into something impossible to even try. I find myself totally unable to attempt anything that might involve the risk of failure. I wind up feeling that even the daily problems of living are too hard to confront, and the lure of my addiction and its offer of temporary relief suddenly seem rational. That's when I should have that warning I often hear in the rooms of my Twelve Step fellowship etched on my forehead: "Poor me. Poor me. Pour me another one."

Maintaining a positive attitude can be difficult for anyone who has been confronted with a problem for which there is no immediate solution. But I must learn above all else not to indulge in self-pity. I may not be able to change or correct the situation immediately, but I can change the attitude I have toward it.

The Eleventh Step enables me to have a power greater than myself to help resolve my problems, large and small. Through prayer and meditation, God rekindles my faith, strengthens my efforts, and makes me feel confident and assured. If I seek the guidance of my Higher Power, I will find no reason to feel sorry for myself ever again.

Prayer

I know, dear God, that when I fall into a bout of self-pity, I am doubting your love and your willingness to help me in all things. Please forgive my lack of faith and instill in me even greater determination to draw closer to you, where I can find comfort and the confidence to face life on life's terms.

Meditation

What am I doing each day to avoid the "poor me's," and what actions do I take when they come over me?

Relaxing in Sobriety

There's something about my addictive personality that makes it difficult for me to relax, mentally or physically. Too often, my mind can't stop running, and it takes my body right along with it. Even the AA slogan I see when I go to meetings—"Easy does it"—doesn't always slow me down.

Part of it is the leftover "self-will run riot" character defect that I dragged with me into recovery. Another part is my tendency to be a perfectionist, someone who has to keep working at whatever it is until it's perfect. When I find myself in that state of mind, I must try to think about another AA principle: "Progress, not perfection."

Diligent practice of the Eleventh Step can help me to slow down and ease up. Through prayer and meditation, when I seek to do the will of my Higher Power each day, I surrender my ways, my wants, and my demands, both on myself and others. I take a deep breath and relax.

Filling my days with too many unnecessary activities leads to stress and tension. This can bring back thoughts of how I used to handle stress in the past by having another drink or drug. I must learn to break the tensions of daily living before they break me. With the help of my Higher Power, I can learn to bend with the stresses and strains of life, like a tree in heavy winds. I can develop the resiliency of spirit to spring erect again after the storm has passed.

I can remember to relax my mind by thinking thoughts of peace, quietness, and tranquility, like mentally picturing a placid mountain lake amid whispering pines, mirroring puffy white clouds in a bright blue sky. I can let my body imitate someone at ease, like a young child building a sand castle or an old man fishing in a drifting rowboat.

I must take the time to exercise—walk, stretch, play golf or tennis, work in the garden—because physical tiredness invites relaxation and sleep. So do the soothing sounds of great music or lying back watching the stars in the night sky.

A face with a frown marks a person under stress, while a face with a smile shows a person at ease and comfortable with life. I should strive to meet life with a sense of humor, learning not to take myself too seriously and even to laugh at myself now and then.

When I'm relaxed, I find it much easier to meditate—to sit and think of all my Higher Power has done for me, all the joy and happiness I've been given in sobriety. The famous poet Ralph Waldo Emerson once wrote concerning such a relaxed meditative state, "Place yourself in the middle of the stream of power and wisdom which animate all whom it floats and you are without effort impelled to truth, to right and a perfect contentment."

Now that I have found a God of my understanding through AA's Twelve Steps of recovery and continue to grow in trust and faith in that Higher Power, relaxed living can be my way of life. A relaxed outlook will help me eliminate confusion and frustration, organize my work, put first things first, do one thing at a time, avoid hurry, and develop a spaciousness of mind and a generosity of spirit.

Living a relaxed life with the help of my Higher Power, a life without serious stress and tension, makes it so much easier to live a spiritual life. And I know I am living a spiritual life when I

- Give all the credit to God's power as a matter of course

- Truly believe that prayer can do anything

- Know in my heart that my happiness and well-being are important to God

- Am comfortable discussing my spiritual beliefs and ideas anywhere and with anyone

- Try to see the presence of God everywhere

When I am relaxed and practicing the Eleventh Step, it's much easier to hear God's voice telling me that my happiness and peace of mind come from letting go, not constantly running to and fro looking for it, seeking it in human haunts and man-made extravaganzas. God's voice tells me to look inside, to witness the changes my Higher Power has wrought in my life by surrendering it to the care of my Creator.

If I work the Eleventh Step on a daily basis, I will see the stress and tension leave my life. I will not only be eager to walk a spiritual path to maintain my sobriety, but I will also be anxious to grab the hand of a new friend in the fellowship and show him or her a path to a wonderful and relaxed new way of life.

Prayer

I now know, dear God, that you have given me this great gift of recovery because my happiness and well-being are important to you. Please give me the grace to stay close to you so that I can avoid all stress and tension, and relax in my sobriety.

Meditation

What do I do in times of stress? What actions do I take to relax and enjoy my sober way of living?

Quality of Sobriety

━━━━━◦●◦━━━━━

I arrived at the doorstep of Alcoholics Anonymous because I was licked. I knew I could no longer go on living with the torture of my addiction. So when God reached out to help me, my first thought was, If I have to give up drinking and drugging to survive and perhaps find a better way to live, I'll try it.

I didn't have a burning desire to stay sober. I only wanted the pain, the fear, the hopelessness to go away. Reluctantly, I became willing to go to any lengths to lose the craving for alcohol and drugs. Gradually, through attending meetings, listening to others, and getting into the Twelve Steps of recovery, the obsession was finally lifted. I now know it was through the grace of God.

When I heard people talking about the "quality of sobriety," I didn't understand until I looked back at my past and compared it with the way I was living in recovery. I began to comprehend that what they really meant was "the quality of a sober life." For my desire to stop drinking had now turned into a desire to live a better life—the kind of life my Higher Power, whom I had found in my Twelve Step program, wanted me to live.

As I continued my sober journey, I discovered help from two important sources. First was my practice of the Eleventh Step. Through prayer and meditation God was inspiring me and enlightening me to take the actions that would improve the quality of my life, that would lead me along a spiritual path. I sought on a daily basis to understand God's will for me and found it was simply to not drink, to practice the Steps of AA, and to help others whenever and wherever I could.

The second source of help was the example of clean and sober Twelve Step fellowship members who were trying to lead a spiritual life. They had lost their insatiable drive for money, power, and prestige. They were no longer seeking fame and honor in order to be praised. As they shared their experience with me, I learned that like them, I don't have to be distinguished in any way in order to be happy and useful. I discovered that being of service to others is its own reward.

I also learned the problems I might face if I followed the example of those who thought "just not drinking" was enough. While some of them did Twelfth Step work, it was mostly getting someone to a meeting or taking someone to an alcohol or drug rehab. But they did it with what some call "gritted-teeth sobriety," which left them little to pass on to newcomers. They hung on by what others call working a "First and Twelfth Step program."

I came to believe what the book *Alcoholics Anonymous* clearly states: that my sobriety is dependent upon my spiritual condition. So if I am to have a quality sober life, I must focus on developing my relationship with my Higher Power and seeking God's will in all things. Self-searching through the Twelve Steps of recovery is the means by which I find new vision, action, and grace to offset the negative side of my nature. It gives me the humility that makes it possible for me to accept God's loving help.

Daily practice of the Eleventh Step is vital if I am to improve the quality of my spiritual life, which is, after all, the basis of my sober life. Seeking God's direction through prayer and meditation enables me to see what I have to change and the actions I must take to do it. One of the suggested prayers of the AA program, the prayer of Saint Francis of Assisi, offers me some candid suggestions in that regard:

> Lord, make me an instrument of your peace. Where there is hatred, let me sow love. Where there is injury, pardon. Where there is doubt, faith. Where there is despair, hope. Where there is darkness, light. Where there is sadness, joy. O Divine Master, grant that I may not so much seek to be consoled as to console, to be understood as to understand, to be loved as to love. For it is in giving that we receive. It is in pardoning that we are pardoned. It is in dying that we are born to eternal life.

Gratitude for my sobriety can best be expressed to my Higher Power by the quality I achieve in my sober life. It's all contained in the last seven words of the Twelfth Step: "practice these principles in all our affairs."

I should strive to meet this goal not only to improve my spiritual life, but also to become a better example to my fellow alcoholics, especially newcomers. I should also do it for myself, to find greater joy and happiness. And I should do it for my Higher Power, who has given me this wonderful sober life through my Twelve Step fellowship. But even with the maximum degree of sobriety in my life, I could never possibly earn all of this on my own merits. It's a gift from God.

Prayer

I believe that my sobriety is totally dependent on my spiritual condition, one day at a time. That's why I beseech you, dear God, for the inspiration and determination to stay close to you through the Eleventh Step. I know that by doing your will each day, I can have a quality sober life.

Meditation

Do I ever think that "just not drinking" is enough, or am I convinced that a strong and growing spiritual life is the only thing that will guarantee my sobriety?

The Serenity Prayer

⟶⟶⟶✦⟵⟵⟵

When I look back at my life before recovery from alcohol and drug addiction, I must admit it was a life filled with indecision and bad judgments. As I've heard so often since joining my Twelve Step program, I had all the answers even though I didn't understand the questions.

How often did I try to climb over a twenty-foot-high wall, always banging my head against it each time I failed? Rarely did I seek another way over it or ask someone else if there might be another way around it. Most important, it never occurred to me that perhaps I was really better off on this side of the wall to begin with.

One of the first things I was handed when I finally started going to meetings was a simple solution to that entire scenario. It's called the Serenity Prayer. I was told it would prove to be one of the most important tools I would have in the struggle against my addiction. As usual, my fellow travelers in recovery were absolutely right:

> God, grant me the serenity to accept the things I cannot change, the courage to change the things I can, and the wisdom to know the difference.

I sought recovery because I was beaten by my addiction. I found victory in defeat. God showed me that the only real source of peace, tranquility, and serenity is in the acceptance of my powerlessness. It's called surrender, or bowing to the inevitable.

And so, as I started along the path of sobriety, I made sure I carried copies of the Serenity Prayer with me at all times and kept copies pasted in my kitchen and bathroom. I learned from firsthand experience why the Serenity Prayer is one of the best-known and most effectively utilized prayers. But all I knew then was that it helped me face, accept, and deal with some of the most difficult problems in my early sobriety. And today it continues to help me deal with life on life's terms.

This wonderful prayer, coupled with the Eleventh Step, gives me the humility, the power, and the wisdom to see God's will each day and the strength and determination to carry it out. It enables me to accept where I am in life at the moment, while continuing to clear away all the debris I can. Whenever I sincerely utter the words, the load I'm carrying drops from my shoulders and the assurance I sense that all will be well brings peace to my soul.

My Higher Power has placed within me the spiritual resources I need to deal effectively with life's challenges. The problem is, these inner resources are often drowned out by the noise and confusion on the outside from the problems and difficulties I sometimes think I have to face all by myself. However, when I ask for help through the Serenity Prayer, God shows me how to use these spiritual resources to calm my fears and take the proper action—or at times simply no action at all.

Bill Wilson, AA's cofounder, recommended the Serenity Prayer to his fledgling band of recovering alcoholics back in

1939, saying it embodies the main principles of the AA recovery program. By simply asking my Higher Power to grant me acceptance, I am admitting my powerlessness over my addiction and recognizing the power of God in my life. When I ask for the courage to change the things I can, I am also asking for direction and guidance, which I find in the Twelve Steps of recovery. And when I seek the wisdom to know what I can or cannot change at the moment, I am turning my will and my life over to the care of my Higher Power. The wisdom I ask for is actually a spiritual awakening that will lead me to an entirely new way to live my life.

The Serenity Prayer is not about doctrine or dogma, as many traditional prayers are. It is, in a sense, a life-skills prayer, a prayer of application and utilization. But it's also, in a much deeper sense, a prayer of ultimate faith. In it I recognize God as the Power greater than myself. I profess my conviction that this Power will grant me the serenity, courage, and wisdom I need to get through the day. Again, this wonderful prayer is not only one of my greatest tools to maintain my sobriety, but one of the most important avenues I have to draw closer to my Higher Power.

Prayer

Let me thank you again, dear God, for the grace to admit and accept my powerlessness over my addiction. Help me to draw closer to you through the Eleventh Step and the Serenity Prayer so that I will continue to have the wisdom and humility to accept and use your healing power in my life.

Meditation

How often do I use the Serenity Prayer when difficulties arise that I cannot handle alone?

WEEK 52

A Spiritual Awakening

It seems like I've been searching all my life, searching for something I never had, searching for something more important than everything else I did have, something that would satisfy the yearning, fill the gap I felt deep inside. I didn't know what I was looking for but I knew I needed to find it in order to have any peace, any meaning, any fulfillment inside myself.

During those terribly lonely times in my life when I felt myself sinking under the weight and torment of my addiction, I would look at other people—happy, smiling, seemingly at ease—and I'd be filled with envy, jealousy, and resentment. It seemed like they had found what I was still searching for, and it angered me.

There were times I even tried what others were doing—working hard, enjoying families, having good relationships, going to church, praying. It didn't work. Nothing gave me any respite except another drink or another drug. Then, after a while, that stopped working, too.

I began to ask myself if I was the only one who trod that path that led to total desperation. Was I the only one who kept asking, seeking, stumbling along that dark and despairing road that had no signs or guideposts? It was a road that led to the top of a cliff. I stood there looking down, fearing I might fall into the abyss. Filled with terror, I called out for help. God came and lifted me up. I was put on a new road, a road that led me to recovery through the Twelve Step program of Alcoholics Anonymous.

Still seeking to fill that gap inside me, I was now given directions—the road map of the Twelve Steps of recovery. I was told the Steps would help me find sobriety, provided I admitted I was powerless over my addiction and turned my will and my life over to the care of a Power greater than myself. That's when a voice deep inside told me that my search was almost over, that what I had been looking for all my life I could now find—a relationship with a loving and caring God of my understanding. I knew it was the beginning of a whole new way of life.

Practicing the Eleventh Step on a daily basis assured me of that. Through prayer and meditation, I drew closer to my Higher Power and came to understand what I had been missing—that I had never really felt loved. Now I did feel loved, unconditionally, by God and by people in my Twelve Step recovery group. At meetings, as I heard the stories of miraculous recovery, the spirituality I had always been looking for began to grow inside. I felt release, gratitude, humility, tolerance, forgiveness, and finally "being at home" with God.

I made a searching and fearless moral inventory, became willing to make amends, cleaned house and repaired the damage, and finally arrived at the Twelfth Step renewed, regenerated, and filled with a spiritual awakening. Willingness, honesty, and open-mindedness marked my sobriety, along with other key signs of a true spiritual awakening:

- An increased tendency to let things happen rather than make them happen

- Frequent attacks of smiling

- Feelings of being connected with others and with nature

- Frequent overwhelming episodes of appreciation

- A tendency to think and act spontaneously

- An unmistakable ability to enjoy the moment

- A loss of interest in conflict

- A loss of interest in judging others

- The ability to love without expecting anything in return

My spiritual awakening, as these signs clearly show, has enabled my life to take on new meaning. I share my experience with others, watch them recover, and see their loneliness vanish as mine did. I now have a host of new friends. My awakening has allowed me to become a useful tool for my Higher Power to help others, which today is a bright spot in my life.

As I look back, my experience has shown me that there was no way I could have found what I had been searching for all my life without first surrendering to my addiction and turning my will and my life over to the care of my loving Higher Power. As a result, my yearning has been satisfied and my life filled with meaning.

Prayer

I am deeply grateful that I now know what I had been searching for and have now found—a loving relationship with you, my Higher Power. Please help me to carry your wonderful message of recovery so that others may find what I've found, a loving and caring God.

Meditation

Do I feel like I have had a spiritual awakening, or do I think I still have more work to do?

The Twelve Steps of Alcoholics Anonymous[5]

1. We admitted we were powerless over alcohol—that our lives had become unmanageable.

2. Came to believe that a Power greater than ourselves could restore us to sanity.

3. Made a decision to turn our will and our lives over to the care of God *as we understood Him*.

4. Made a searching and fearless moral inventory of ourselves.

5. Admitted to God, to ourselves, and to another human being the exact nature of our wrongs.

6. Were entirely ready to have God remove all these defects of character.

7. Humbly asked Him to remove our shortcomings.

8. Made a list of all persons we had harmed, and became willing to make amends to them all.

9. Made direct amends to such people wherever possible, except when to do so would injure them or others.

10. Continued to take personal inventory and when we were wrong promptly admitted it.

11. Sought through prayer and meditation to improve our conscious contact with God *as we understood Him,* praying only for knowledge of His will for us and the power to carry that out.

12. Having had a spiritual awakening as the result of these steps, we tried to carry this message to alcoholics, and to practice these principles in all our affairs.

Notes

1. *Alcoholics Anonymous,* 4th ed. (New York: Alcoholics Anonymous World Services, Inc., 2001), 44–45.

2. Borchert, William G. *The Lois Wilson Story: When Love Is Not Enough.* (Center City, MN: Hazelden, 2005), 302.

3. *Alcoholics Anonymous,* 4th ed. (New York: Alcoholics Anonymous World Services, Inc., 2001), 63.

4. *Alcoholics Anonymous,* 4th ed. (New York: Alcoholics Anonymous World Services, Inc., 2001), 83–84.

5. *Alcoholics Anonymous,* 4th ed. (New York: Alcoholics Anonymous World Services, Inc., 2001), 59–60.

About Hazelden Publishing

As part of the Hazelden Betty Ford Foundation, Hazelden Publishing offers both cutting-edge educational resources and inspirational books. Our print and digital works help guide individuals in treatment and recovery, and their loved ones. Professionals who work to prevent and treat addiction also turn to Hazelden Publishing for evidence-based curricula, digital content solutions, and videos for use in schools, treatment programs, correctional programs, and electronic health records systems. We also offer training for implementation of our curricula.

Through published and digital works, Hazelden Publishing extends the reach of healing and hope to individuals, families, and communities affected by addiction and related issues.

For more information about Hazelden publications,
please call **800-328-9000**
or visit us online at **hazelden.org/bookstore.**

Other titles that may interest you:

Twenty-Four Hours a Day

Since 1954, *Twenty-Four Hours a Day* has become a stable force in the recovery of many alcoholics throughout the world. This book offers daily thoughts, meditations, and prayers for living a clean and sober life.
Softcover, 400 pp.
Order No. 5093

A Program for You

A Guide to the Big Book's Design for Living
A Program for You interprets the original AA program as described in the book *Alcoholics Anonymous* and provides readers with a thorough understanding of Twelve Step principles.
Softcover, 192 pp.
Order No. 5122

The 12 Step Prayer Book, Volume 1

A Collection of Favorite 12 Step Prayers and Inspirational Readings
Written and Compiled by Bill P. and Lisa D.
Words of wisdom and inspiration, gleaned from Twelve Step meetings and adapted from common prayers and devotional readings, fill this popular prayer book.
Softcover, 160 pp.
Order No. 2367

The 12 Step Prayer Book, Volume 2

More 12 Step Prayers and Inspirational Readings
Written and Compiled by Bill P. and Lisa D.
Readers will find a prayer to inspire each new day in recovery with this second volume of our popular book of devotionals.
Softcover, 138 pp.
Order No. 2911

Hazelden books are available at fine bookstores everywhere. To order directly from Hazelden, call 800-328-9000 or visit hazelden.org/bookstore.